# WHAT EVERY VIRGINIA WOMAN
# NEEDS TO KNOW ABOUT DIVORCE

# WHAT EVERY VIRGINIA WOMAN NEEDS TO KNOW ABOUT DIVORCE

SHEERA R. HERRELL, Esquire, CFP™

&

KATHERINE WILCOX CARTER, Esquire
*www.hoflaw.com*

# WARNING AND DISCLAIMER

This book is in the nature of general information, not specific legal advice.  Please use this book for informational purposes only.

# Table of Contents

# WHO IS BEHIND THIS BOOK AND WHY SHOULD I LISTEN TO THE AUTHORS?

Relax. Slow down. Breathe. It's going to be okay. The prospect of going through a divorce may seem daunting but take a deep breath and begin the process one baby step at a time.

We see women through this process every single day, and one of the things that we love the most is seeing our clients transform. After all, there's no prize for staying in an abusive, unhappy, unfulfilling, or unrewarding relationship – but there can be a lot to be gained by taking your life back and making your future more like the life you envision for yourself.

If you are a woman contemplating or confronting divorce, you don't have to do it alone. Help is readily available. We're here to educate you about your rights and entitlements under Virginia law. We want you to know:

1. The different and distinctive ways you can resolve your divorce.

2. That truly effective professionals abound in our community who can help you organize and structure your life into manageable parts so that your divorce does not seem so daunting and overwhelming.

3. That understanding the laws that govern divorce and understanding the process of divorce helps relieve the stress of divorce. Knowledge is power!

## CHARLIE AND KRISTEN HOFHEIMER
## -THE ORIGINAL TRAILBLAZERS-

This book has been modified from its original version, which was previously written by Charlie and Kristen Hofheimer, a father-daughter team, and the original 'women-only' family law attorneys in Virginia.

Back in 1992, Charlie Hofheimer founded the Hofheimer Family Law Firm after he noticed that women needed more help than they were getting in their family law cases.

Charlie's daughter, Kristen Hofheimer, joined the firm a few short years later, and, together, the two built up the firm into what it is today — the largest Virginia family law firm dedicated to representing women exclusively.

Though things have changed significantly since 1992, we still find that there's a distinct need for women to have specific representation in the Virginia court system.

Why? It's a good question, and one we have to answer all the time! (You wouldn't believe how many men call our office and yell at us about discrimination and the Constitution and their rights!)

**Why do women need dedicated legal representation in divorce and custody cases?**

The reason that we believe — to this very day — that women need dedicated legal representation in family law cases is because, historically at least, men made more money and had the ability to finance an attorney more easily than a woman. Though women earn more than they used to and work full time more often than in other generations, there is still a wage gap. Women still earn only 81 cents on the dollar to what men earn; for women of color, the chasm is even greater.

**But, why women only? Why wouldn't a law firm want to dedicate itself to representing the higher wage earners?**

In just our area, there are TWO law firms that represent men only; however, there is only one in all of Virginia (as of the time of this writing) that represents women only.

But that also explains the need for us, occupying our own space. Sure, there are people "dedicated" to representing the advantaged few. It's really not hard to do, is it? But, on the other side, there really does have to be someone dedicated to representing the underdog. Maybe using the word "underdog" is being a bit dramatic; we don't want you to have the wrong impression. In actuality, we don't think women are necessarily disadvantaged in the courts by virtue of their sex as much as we think that they are economically disadvantaged before they even get to the doors of the courthouse.

It's hard to finance, say, a spousal support case against a higher wage-earning husband; he can outspend you on the litigation before you even get in front of a judge. He can note an appeal that you can't afford, too. He can even hire an attorney more easily, without fear of not being able to make the retainer fee. In some cases, as well, he may even consult with a number of the top area attorneys, without even intending to hire one of them, simply so that they are conflicted out of representing his wife. It takes money (and time, not to mention a pinch of narcissism) to do this, but we see it happen.

**We're not man-haters. We're woman supporters and we believe that, when women have a place at the table, the outcomes are better for children and families.**

Back in his day, Charlie Hofheimer campaigned to have women admitted at his alma mater, Washington & Lee University School of Law, before returning to his hometown to start teaching seminars every Second Saturday of the month about What Virginia Women Need to Know About Divorce. It wasn't until later that he opened the law firm, but, today, we've been in existence for over thirty years.

Kristen Hofheimer attended law school after her divorce at the University of Virginia, with her then one year old son in tow. That's unusual today; in her time, it was virtually unheard of. She started a mother's childcare cooperative, and even wrote a law review article (still relevant and referenced today!) about breastfeeding in custody and visitation cases. She joined the practice with her father, working extensively with protective mothers' groups and handling complex custody and visitation matters.

Charlie retired, and Kristen passed away in 2019 at the age of 49 after a long struggle with breast cancer – leaving the rest of us, but especially Sheera Herrell, who took over ownership of the firm, to carry on.

Today, as all women ourselves, and as mothers and professionals, we identify with our clients. We sympathize with their concerns and, in many ways, personify them. But it's not so much about us as it is about the world we inhabit, and in lifting up other women to support us all.

It's about providing education and empowerment, so that women feel that they have the information available to them to make the best decisions possible. It's about protecting them from lashing out emotionally, or out of blinding fear, by ensuring that the intelligence they have is up to date, accurate, Virginia specific, and designed to lead them to a better happy ever after.

It's about being able to make consistent, well formed, logical arguments to the court. Other attorneys have to talk out of both sides of their mouths, defending dad in one case and mom in the next. Our arguments are coherent, cohesive, and consistent because we're continually pointing out the same things, dealing with the same shortcomings, and addressing the same concerns.

When it comes to lawyers, there are those who practice in many areas (wills and estates, family law, personal injury) and become a 'jack of all trades'. With the law, it can be hard to keep up with changes, updates, best practices, and case law across many areas. Similarly, it's hard to represent men and women. The other side is a distraction, and our focus on *just* family law and *just* women allows us to do a better job across the board.

But ultimately, we represent women because we believe in it.

**Our goals are lofty: (1) to provide up to date, Virginia-specific information to Virginia women about family law, (2) to empower through our supportive community, and (3) to provide top-notch legal representation, in and out of the courtroom.**

There is a lot at stake in a family law cases. Very few things touch your life as intimately or have implications as far reaching as a divorce or custody case, and it is important to have an attorney by your side that is prepared to do what it takes to help get you the results you need. In a day and age where attorneys face complaints for failing to respond to emails, for being unprepared in court, for mansplaining and talking down to their clients without understanding (or caring) about their actual proprieties, we're...different. We think that matters.

We're determined to carry the Hofheimer's legacy into the future. Their original book was a major source of inspiration in this rewritten version. Though they're no longer practicing with us, we couldn't begin this book without offering our thoughts on where we've come from. It's as important to us as where we are going, and it informs all of the things we do and the decisions we make.

Thank you for your legacy, Charlie & Kristen. We miss you!

4

## WHO/WHAT IS HOFHEIMER FAMILY LAW FIRM?

Back in 1991, Charlie Hofheimer recognized the need for a law firm representing women only in family law cases. At the time, he had already started teaching the *Second Saturday: What Every Virginia Woman Needs to Know About Divorce* seminars, which helped to show him the distinct disadvantage that women face in the court systems.

Already a sort-of pioneer for women's rights after campaigning to have them admitted to his alma mater, Washington and Lee University School of Law, it was a very authentic fit.

Over the years, more and more lawyers joined up with Charlie and the Hofheimer Family Law Firm was born. After his daughter, Kristen, joined the firm, it became clear that she would be the natural predecessor.

Together with Charlie's wife, Diane, who worked as Kristen's paralegal, the trio took on increasingly challenging custody cases, working with many protective moms' groups. Charlie and Kristen were both sought-after speakers who gained a lot of respect in the field.

They were top notch litigators, too, neither backed down from a fight – though they each handled their battles differently. Charlie was aggressive, fist pounding, and dramatic; Kristen was softer spoken, fiercely intelligent, and incredibly quick on her feet.

At the same time that Kristen graduated law school and started with the firm, Sheera Herrell joined too, and quickly became a part of the family. Often referring to the two as his "good daughter" (Sheera) and his "bad daughter" (Kristen), Charlie affectionately ribbed them (and everyone else) in the office.

Charlie wrote our most popular title, and the precursor to this new edition of *What Every Virginia Woman Needs to Know about Divorce* and maintained our monthly divorce seminar program. He was convinced that the way forward was to make sure that every Virginia woman facing a divorce or custody case had the information at her disposal to make the hard decisions.

During her time at the helm, Kristen wrote the first edition of our Women's Custody Survival Guide, created the Custody

Bootcamp for Moms seminar, and kickstarted the popular Girl's Night Out event series.

Kristen retired in 2017 after she was diagnosed with breast cancer for a second time. Charlie had retired shortly before, and they moved to "Hofheimer Holler" in the mountains of North Carolina with Charlie's wife Diane, their son RD and his two children, Kristen's wife, Missy, Kristen's son, Shay and his wife, Morgan, and their newborn son, Nova. Kristen passed away, surrounded by her family, in January of 2019.

Kristen's illness and sudden departure changed things for the firm, who had always been united under the Hofheimer's overall vision for the future.

That's when Sheera took over. By that time, she had been practicing with the firm for nearly 20 years. She is collaboratively trained, and is a Certified Financial Planner, so we knew she would bring amazing things to the firm.

Though it's still early in her "reign", we've already weathered a worldwide pandemic, moved our divorce seminar to an online-only format, and updated this and many of our other online resources.

The world – and the practice of law – is changing. But the need for women, regardless of their socioeconomic status, to have dedicated, exclusive representation is constant.

For more information on Virginia divorce, please visit
*www.hoflaw.com*

For more information about our monthly "What Every Virginia
Woman Needs to Know About Divorce" seminars, please visit
*www.monthlydivorceseminar.com*

For more information on custody issues, please visit
*www.custodyseminar.com*

## OUR PROMISE TO YOU!

We're here for you! It's our goal to make sure that you have all the information you need to make the big decisions about how to move your case forward.

Certainly, after reading this, you'll have more information than 99% of divorcing men – and that's a start! But you also have a unique set of circumstances and your own specific concerns that may or may not be covered here. We encourage you to attend our monthly divorce seminar and, if custody is an issue, one of our upcoming *Custody Bootcamp for Mom* seminars, too.

Our seminars are taught by our attorneys and give you the opportunity to ask your questions live, too, so it's a great place to ask for clarification or about that thing that has kept you lying awake at night.

If you haven't visited our website at www.hoflaw.com, please do so and make sure to check out our library of resources, as well as our extensive list of books and free reports, all available for your use.

If you still need specific questions answered, it may be time to consider a consultation.

We're committed to helping you have the answers you need!

# LET'S GET STARTED

## THE BARE BASICS

### What is divorce?  Who can get one?

Divorce is the legal process of ending a valid marriage.

In a divorce, all the rights and responsibilities of the parties have to be divided between them, either by order of the court or by agreement of the parties.  This includes division of assets and liabilities, as well as a determination of child and/or spousal support, and custody and visitation.

Anyone who is legally married can get a divorce.  Divorce does not require the consent of both spouses.  (Though a non-consenting spouse can make things more difficult and, ultimately, more time consuming for both parties.)

### How do you resolve a divorce?

In Virginia, you can resolve a divorce in 2 ways: (1) in court, by order of a judge; and (2) by negotiating a signed agreement between the parties.

### What are the different types of divorce?

Divorces can be either contested, uncontested, and fault or no-fault. The way these terms relate to each other says a lot about the type of divorce – including how long it'll take, how much it'll cost, and, ultimately, how good the results will be.

### Contested v. Uncontested

Contested and uncontested refer to whether or not you and your spouse are able to reach an agreement.

Uncontested means that you and your husband have signed an agreement, and that there are no disagreements as it relates to equitable distribution (the way the property will be divided), custody and visitation, or support.

That's not to say that it's *easy* to get an agreement in place. It's often really challenging! But whether you can get there in the end or not is the difference between a contested and an uncontested divorce.

A contested divorce means that the two of you ultimately weren't able to reach an agreement on all issues. You may be able to agree on some things, but if even one issue is contested, you'll have to go to court to let the judge decide and your case will be considered contested.

Contested and uncontested *do not* refer to whether or not the parties 'agree' to the divorce itself; it refers only to whether you've agreed about how the assets and liabilities will ultimately be divided.

## Fault v. No-fault

Fault and no-fault refer to your grounds for divorce. In Virginia, you must have grounds in order to get a divorce, so you'll have to choose one to use.

## Fault-based Grounds for Divorce

When you use fault grounds for divorce, you're basically alleging that some fault or bad act of the other party ultimately led to the breakdown of the marriage.

In Virginia, there are 6 fault-based grounds that you can use: adultery (which also includes sodomy and buggery), cruelty, apprehension of bodily hurt, desertion, abandonment, and felony conviction.

## Adultery, Sodomy, and Buggery

The sexual grounds – adultery, sodomy, and buggery – are all grouped together.

Technically, adultery is when a married person knowingly has sex with someone who is not his or her spouse. When we say "sex", we include oral, anal, and vaginal sex. (Sorry to get graphic!)

Adultery is NOT anything else – dating, hugging, kissing, hand holding, etc.

Technically, adultery must be proved by clear and convincing evidence, and you'll also need a corroborating witness (someone like an ex-girlfriend, or a private investigator) to support your allegations.

### IMPORTANT

There are two other important things you should know about adultery cases.

1.  Adultery is an absolute bar to spousal support.

If you've committed adultery, that is an absolute bar to receiving spousal support. Of course, that's assuming you would have received it anyway. But it's worth keeping in mind.

There is an exception in cases where "manifest injustice" would result, but that would be both expensive and time consuming to prove.

2.  If you have sex with him after finding out that he's committed adultery, you've legally forgiven him!

Once you know about the adultery, having sex with him means that you legally forgive the adultery.

You only forgive the acts of adultery that you know about, so if there are others that he hasn't confessed to, or if he goes on to commit acts of adultery with the same or another person, you haven't forgiven those other acts.

It works in reverse, too. If you've committed adultery and he has sex with you after he finds out about it, he's forgiven you, too.

When adultery is legally forgiven, that means that you can no longer use adultery for your grounds of divorce. If you do, your spouse could then use "condonation" as an affirmative defense, and either plead something in the alternative or ask that your complaint be dismissed. If a subsequent incident of adultery occurs, you can file on that subsequent incident as long as you do not legally forgive your spouse again.

If a subsequent incident of adultery does not occur, it just means you'll have to find alternate grounds; keep in mind that you can always use no-fault grounds if you don't have different fault-based grounds to use.

Legally forgiving adultery does not erase the adultery for purposes of spousal support, though – so getting him to have sex have sex with you after you commit adultery won't restore your ability to ask for spousal support from him!

## "Immediate" Divorce: When you can plead (and prove) adultery

There's only one situation where you can get an immediate divorce, and that's where you can allege and prove, by clear and convincing evidence, adultery.

Still, as far as fault-based divorces go, only adultery (and sodomy and buggery, because they're all lumped together under the adultery heading) qualifies you for a so-called immediate divorce.

All of the fault-based grounds allow you to *file* for divorce immediately, but only adultery allows you to move forward with the divorce proceedings immediately.

## So, if I can allege and prove adultery, I can get an immediate divorce?

Yes. Well, technically, you can get an immediate divorce, anyway. In reality, it usually doesn't work like that because it's actually fairly complicated.

## What do I need to know or do to allege adultery in my divorce complaint?

In order to allege adultery, you don't need to be able to prove it right away. You just need to have a reasonable belief that your grounds exist. Normally, when we file a complaint based on adultery, we allege the information that we have. Ideally, we'll use the date (on or about) when the adultery occurred, the location, and the initials of the alleged paramour, if we have them.

That's enough to get into court, but you'll need to do a lot more to prove adultery to the satisfaction of the judge.

## How do you prove adultery?

Adultery, because it's still a crime in Virginia and potentially carries significant criminal and civil penalties, is the hardest to prove of all the fault-based grounds for divorce.

To prove adultery, you have to do so by "clear and convincing evidence." It's a fairly difficult standard to meet, and you'll have to provide a corroborating witness, too.

## What's a corroborating witness?

A corroborating witness is a person who can testify that your grounds exist. Usually, in an adultery case, we'll use someone like a private investigator.

We don't have to actually catch them, on camera or video, having sex, but we do have to prove that, in all likelihood, sex happened. We can normally do this by having a private investigator tail your husband. The private investigator can watch him as he goes about his business, goes into a hotel or his (or his paramour's) home, and then watch all the exits. If he can catch your husband emerging the next morning, you've probably got a pretty good case.

Still, as you can probably imagine, it's pretty expensive to hire a private investigator. There are often a lot of hours involved, trying to catch him at something inappropriate. It's difficult to know, ahead of time, exactly how hard it will be, or how much of the private investigator's time will be wrapped up in trying to gather evidence.

## It sounds easy! My husband cheated. Can I get an immediate divorce?

Okay, so, here's the thing. Even though, if you can prove adultery, you do qualify for an immediate divorce, most attorneys don't push these things forward quite so quickly. Why? Well, there's some risk involved.

Imagine this... You file for divorce, using adultery as your grounds, and you schedule a trial as quickly as you can.

### Problem #1

You may not be able to schedule it all that quickly anyway. Most courts have a lot of procedural requirements (roadblocks, essentially) in place to slow you down and encourage you and your husband to settle, rather than leaving it up to a judge to decide. You may have to have a judicial settlement conference, attend mediation, and prepare pretrial documents first—which can take time. In addition, like we've already discussed, you may have to wait a little while before your private investigator has enough evidence to move your case forward.

Besides that, most courts are pretty backed up. In Virginia Beach, you won't be able to even get a trial date for 8 or 9 months; it's just not possible to schedule sooner.

Even though you qualify for an immediate divorce, that doesn't mean you can jump ahead in line. The cases that were filed first and already had hearings or trials scheduled are going to be handled before the judge gets to yours.

### Problem #2

What happens if you can't prove adultery? Really, this is the biggest problem. You can gather all the proof in the world, but it's ultimately up to the judge to determine whether your evidence, exhibits, and testimony is sufficiently clear and convincing. If you can't convince him, then what?

That's a major problem. If the judge isn't convinced by your testimony, you don't have grounds and you can't get divorced.

If you waited until your one year of separation was up before your trial, if you weren't able to prove adultery, you could use no-fault grounds instead. If you try to move forward for that immediate divorce and then you can't prove it, you're out of luck entirely. That means your divorce will be denied, your case dismissed, and you're back at square one.

Not only are you not divorced, but everything you've done so far is wasted. You'll have to file for divorce all over again, using the same or different grounds, and you'll start again from the beginning. All the time and money you've invested in your adultery case is gone; you'll pay from the beginning all over again.

As an attorney, this is a situation to avoid at all costs. Most attorneys, regardless of how good the proof is, would want to wait until the year was up to have that final divorce trial. Why? Well, imagine how unhappy a client would be, after taking all that time and spending all that money to get up to trial, only to be unsuccessful in even getting a divorce. And to return to the beginning of the process, despite all the money spent already, and have virtually nothing done. It's pretty much the worst possible scenario–for attorney and, especially, for the client.

### Does that mean I can't use my adultery grounds?

No. You definitely can, if that's something you want to do. We definitely recommend that you talk to an attorney in advance, though, to make a decision about whether it's worth it to pursue in your unique case.

There's more to discuss than whether you want to file for divorce immediately or whether you'll wait the whole year; ultimately, the real discussion is whether the juice is worth the squeeze. Will pursuing adultery ensure that your divorce moves forward the way you hope? Will you get what you need to start over? Will you spend too much on attorney's fees, and then wind up with a larger share of a smaller pie? Or will it prove to be the thing that makes your case that much better? Because a judge *can* award one side a disproportionate amount of the assets because of their negative nonmonetary contribution to the marriage. (That's lawyer speak for "if he's bad, it's possible you could get more".)

### Cruelty and Apprehension of Bodily Hurt

Cruelty and apprehension of bodily hurt are the domestic violence grounds.

Though people use all sorts of abuse to file their complaint using these grounds and get in to court, including verbal and emotional abuse, in order to actually prove this to the satisfaction of the judge and get your divorce granted on either of these grounds, you'll likely need some evidence of actual physical harm.

Domestic violence is often one of those things that is incredibly hard to prove. There often aren't witnesses (or if there are, they're the children, and we don't like to make children testify in court). Physical evidence, too, can be difficult to come by.

In some cases, we have police reports, or medical records, which can mean that it's possible to get a doctor to testify to the abuse.

Victims of domestic violence, though, often don't go through "official" channels, press charges, or go to the hospital.

Still, as is often the case, there can be reasons that you might want to file on these grounds, even if you ultimately know that you can't finalize using them.

### Desertion and Abandonment

Desertion and abandonment are often lumped together, too.

The physical act of desertion is one spouse leaving the marital residence without the consent of the other spouse. If there is an agreement between the parties that one spouse moves out, that is not desertion.

### What if I want to leave the marital residence? What if he does? Is it desertion or abandonment?

If you want to leave the marital residence, it's often best to get an agreement in place prior to leaving that says that the two of you agree that you can go and that your leaving will not constitute abandonment or desertion of the marriage. If he wants to leave, we would suggest that you talk to an attorney ahead of time, but ideally you'd get at least a temporary agreement in place that would specify how the rent or mortgage and utilities and other expenses will be paid in the future.

If you do actually leave, with or without an agreement in place, you should always take the kids.

### What if there's domestic violence?

In general, we would never advise that you stay in a situation that is physically dangerous for you or your children.

### IMPORTANT: Constructive Desertion

In a domestic violence situation, you could use constructive desertion as your grounds. It's a little tricky because you technically have to file your complaint with the court *on the day that you leave* the house, but it essentially forestalls his ability to use your "desertion" or "abandonment" against you if you have sufficient facts to allege desertion.

You can use constructive desertion in a case where he made the living situation in the home so bad that no reasonable person could have stayed.

17

If you want to use constructive desertion as your grounds, you will likely need to speak with a divorce and custody attorney in advance to set your plans in motion.

## What if I've already left the home and I didn't use constructive desertion?

Could he use it, if you left without an agreement, without leave of court, without a protective order, and without you filing first on constructive desertion? Yes. Will it matter? Probably not but we can't promise that is won't.

Don't panic. Your safety and well-being are first and foremost, so if you've left the home, you really shouldn't waste time worrying. Schedule an appointment with a licensed, experienced Virginia divorce and custody attorney sooner rather than later, and we'll help you figure out your next steps. However, making a plan with attorney before leaving your home is your best plan.

## How do I get him out of the house?

Of all the issues we will discuss, this is among the toughest to answer. Absent provable abuse entitling you to a Protective Order issued by a Juvenile and Domestic Relations District Court, you can t make him leave and most judges in probably won't kick him out. Adjust accordingly for the time being.

## Why can't I kick him out of the house? He is making life miserable for me and the kids!

Perhaps no issue is more frustrating and toxic than when a family is headed for divorce, and you want your husband out of the home.

There are simply no easy answers to resolve this matter. The courts are very reluctant to forcefully remove anyone from his home unless there is very clear evidence of physical threat/abuse.

The underlying reason for this goes back to the old English common law that your home is your castle, and the king was unable to enter your home absent a writ from the court.

Again, adjust accordingly, with the long-term picture in mind. Keep in mind, your husband may be trying to get you to leave the marital home and you may need counsel as to whether you should leave and when and how you would leave. You do not want to leave without a jointly agreed upon strategy with your attorney.

## Felony Conviction

If either you or your husband has been convicted of a felony for which you could serve a year or more in prison, that's also grounds for divorce. (Probably the easiest one to prove, too!)

## No-fault Grounds for Divorce

Moving forward with your divorce on "no-fault" doesn't technically mean there was no-fault. There's no requirement that you use your fault-based grounds if you have them; it's entirely up to you whether you choose to move forward with fault grounds, if you have them, or choose no-fault grounds instead.

No-fault means that you have decided to move forward with your divorce using your period of separation as your grounds for divorce. That may mean that you don't have fault-based grounds to use, but, more likely, it means that you've decided to move forward with the divorce without regard for the other party's fault.

## Why would I move forward on no-fault grounds if I have fault grounds I can use?

That's a good question! Fault-based grounds for divorce have to be proven. Depending on which grounds you use, you'll have to meet a specific burden of proof when your case goes to court.

Many people *file* on fault, if they have the grounds, but usually it's as a means to an end – either to get support established, to be able to conduct discovery, or for some other reason. But filing on fault isn't the same thing as *proving* to the satisfaction of the judge that your grounds exist.

Proving that your grounds exist is expensive and time consuming. Though the Virginia Equitable Distribution statute allows the judge to consider the "negative non-monetary contributions" of each party, and to award one spouse or the other a disproportionate amount of the assets, it doesn't often happen – at least, not just because they, for example, committed adultery.

Ultimately, it usually comes down to whether the juice is worth the squeeze. If you're going to make your case cost more money and take more time, you probably want to know that the investment is going to pay dividends for you, right? In most cases, the answer is no – so, most of the time, people end up moving forward with no-fault divorces.

As always, though, it's a heavily fact specific decision to make, so you should go through your options one-on-one with a licensed Virginia divorce attorney before making any big decisions about your case!

## Fault v. No-fault, Contested v. Uncontested

There are essentially three different categories of divorce, listed below. We'll walk through each one and discuss what's involved.

It's important that you understand these distinctions at the beginning of your case because your choices now will shape your case as it moves forward. The more you know, the better your choices can be.

To the extent that you can establish goals and priorities now, your ability to understand your options and consistently make decisions that are in line with your goals will help get you the results you want.

### Contested Fault Divorce

In a contested fault-based divorce, you do not have an agreement about how the assets and liabilities will be divided *and* you have to prove your fault-based grounds exist.

When you litigate, you'll have to introduce evidence, witnesses, and exhibits both to support your argument for how your assets and liabilities should be divided and also to establish your grounds.

### Contested No-fault Divorce

In a contested no-fault divorce, you do not have an agreement about how your assets and liabilities will be divided, but you've decided to move your case forward on no-fault grounds.

Just because you use no-fault grounds does not mean you and your spouse can agree about how everything should be divided. It's also possible that your spouse may move forward with a fault base divorce even if you are moving forward with a no fault divorce.

When you litigate, you will spend the bulk of your time introducing evidence, witnesses, and exhibits to support your argument for how the assets and liabilities will be divided.

Your no-fault grounds, meaning that you've been separated for the statutory period, can be much more simply proven by your own testimony. There is a burden of proof, but it's nowhere near as difficult as proving that your fault-based grounds exist.

### Uncontested No-Fault Divorce

In an uncontested no-fault divorce, you and your spouse ultimately were able to reach an agreement about how your assets and liabilities will be divided, and you've agreed to move forward using no-fault grounds.

In an uncontested no-fault divorce, you don't have to go to court at all. There's no litigation.

The terms of your divorce are exactly what you agree to in a negotiated, signed separation agreement. That's not saying that reaching an agreement is easy, but you don't leave anything up to a judge.

In a separation agreement, your only limitation is your own creativity and what you can get the other side to agree to do. You have a lot more flexibility and aren't limited to what a judge can do.

As far as your grounds are concerned, one of you will have to testify – and that will be that.

## Uncontested Fault Divorce

An uncontested *fault* divorce – there's no such thing!

There is no such thing as agreeing in a separation agreement that, for example, one of you committed adultery. For any of the fault-based grounds, you'll have to provide evidence and meet a specific burden of proof – which you cannot do in an agreement.

A fault-based divorce requires litigation!

## Legal Separation in Virginia

It's important to understand the divorce itself, but separation is the first part of the process.

There are often a lot of questions when it comes to separation, and most of it comes down to a difference in how we use the word "separation" in regular language, and what attorneys mean when they talk about legal separation. There's a difference!

When regular people talk about being separated, they may mean that they're taking a break to think about their marriage. In many cases, it's a separation with the hopes of a future reconciliation. It may include actual physical separation from the home, but it may not.

It often includes marriage counseling, too.

When lawyers use the word separation, it is different. The phrase 'legal separation' is not a technical legal status in Virginia. . Though there are no forms to sign or anything that needs to happen with the court, being separated means that two things have happened:

1. One spouse has formed the intent to end the marriage, and

2. The parties stop cohabitating.

Let's look into these in a little more detail because these concepts are important.

## Forming the intent to end the marriage

The first component of a legal separation is forming the intent to end the marriage. Only one of you needs to form the intent to end it, but the intent has to be there.

You're saying, "That's it, I'm done, and I'm for real this time!" In your mind, at the time, there are no ifs, ands, or buts about it. It's completely over.

People who think that their marriages are completely over are not hoping for a reconciliation or continuing to attend marriage counseling. What would the point of marriage counseling be if it's completely over?

That doesn't mean you can't reconcile later, it just means that, at the time the intent was formed, you were not considering reconciliation as a possibility.

## Stop Cohabitating

"Cohabitation" is a fancy legal word we use to describe when two people live together as husband and wife.

When you stop "live together as husband and wife," you stop cooking and cleaning for each other. You don't grocery shop for each other. You don't eat dinner together.

It's how you behave both inside and outside of the home. Outside of the home, you don't wear wedding rings, attend parties or events or church together, or present yourselves with a united front.

As much as possible, you should live the way you would if you lived in completely separate physical spaces – though that's not necessarily required.

Once you've formed the intent to end the marriage, you should also stop cohabitating. These things should come together at a specific moment in time – and that's the point at which you and your spouse are formally legally separated.

## Can we be separated while living in the same house?

In many cases, yes – though you should know that the judge may look at your case a little more critically when the time comes to finalize your divorce. In fact, in some jurisdictions, you'll actually have to have an in-person ore tenus hearing to finalize your divorce!

I say yes but with reservations. You'll obviously want to make sure that you're doing absolutely everything you can to show that you are as separated as you can possibly be.

As a litmus test, a general rule of thumb is to ask yourself: "Would I be doing this if we actually lived in completely separate physical spaces?" If the answer is no, well, that's a good sign that you shouldn't be doing it.

## But what about sex?

Well, that's the million-dollar question. Obviously, it's best if you don't. If you are living separate and apart in the same residence, having sex with your spouse would be very good evidence to prove the parties have not actually separated. And, if there's any question at all about his having committed adultery, from a sexual health standpoint, you really shouldn't. (And if you're worried about where he's been, it's never a bad idea to get tested – just in case!)

Sex, on its own, probably doesn't defeat your claim that you're separated (if you are living in different homes) – unless you do it with some kind of intent towards reconciliation.

Still, it's risky. Though it's unlikely that a judge will ask you specifically about your sex life during your period of separation, it's possible – and you'll be testifying, whether by affidavit or at an in-person ore tenus hearing, under penalty of perjury. This is probably a case of "reasonable minds may differ" in terms of judges' feelings about sex while separated.

If you do intend to live separate under the same roof, follow these guidelines:

## Guidelines for Separation Under the Same Roof

- Use separate bedrooms.

- Do not engage in romantic or sexual intimacy.

- Each spouse should shop for his or her own food, prepare his or her own meals; should not shop for the other, including clothing and other necessities.

- Do not use the other spouses food or other purchases.

- Do not eat meals together (exceptions: holidays or childrens birthdays).

- Each spouse should be responsible for caring for his or

23

her own space within the home.

- Each spouse should do his or her own laundry.
- Use a separate and secure computer. Still, be careful what you use the computer for.
- Use a separate and secure telephone/cell phone for personal and business calls.
- Establish separate checking accounts.
- Cease socializing together, e.g., do not attend parties, movies, theater, etc. together.
- Do not attend church together.
- When there are minor children, interact as parents only where strictly necessary from the children's perspective and their well-being, e.g., it would be acceptable for the parents to go together to a meeting with a school official relative to problems confronting a particular child, but less appropriate for the parents to ride together and sit together at a child's school play or soccer game.
- Cease gift giving between spouses for such occasions as birthdays, Christmas, anniversary, Valentine's Day, etc.
- Make known to close associates, relatives, etc. that you are not living as man and wife but are separated within the residence.
- Have an objective third party come to the home from time to time to personally observe the two spouse's separate and distinct living quarters (bedrooms, bathrooms, etc.).
- Utilize separate entrances to the residence if feasible.
- Be prepared to explain reasons for living separately under the same roof, e.g., financial considerations; unavailability of separate residence; easing children's transition to parental separation, etc.
- Do not role play as the happy couple in front of neighbors and social acquaintances. You cannot 'hold yourselves out" as husband and wife to the community

**REMINDER:** We said it once, but we're going to say it one more time: lving separately within the same residence as your spouse can be very difficult to prove to a judge. You may discover that the judge will not accept "your separate under the same roof" status and tell you to come back after a year of living separately in your own residences. This could pose an added expense as well as a delay to your divorce process.

The reason for this warning is that it is clear the courts do not favor "living in the same residence" separations, and most judges will not award a divorce relying on an in-home separation; however, there are reported cases where judges have permitted separation under the same roof, provided that many, if not all, of the conditions indicated in the checklist are followed.

This is also one of those things that sort of goes in and out of fashion. There was a period of time where the judges were very strict, then a period of relative laxity – but, recently, judges seem to have returned to their former, stricter mindset when it comes to living separate in the same home.

If you have any questions or concerns about your status, it's a good idea to talk to an attorney about them so that you can come up with a game plan that helps you get divorced successfully without extra delays!

### How your "separation" looks matters: confusing cohabitation, collusion, and public policy.

In Virginia, "cohabitation" is living together as if married.

This does not mean that you have to be having sex with your husband in order to be deemed a family in the eyes of the law.

Just because you have not been intimate for a while does not mean that the two aren't cohabiting. That's why we say that when you're living separate in the same home, you're behaving – both inside of it and outside of it – as people who are not married.

Often, couples do not want their friends to know that they are getting separated or divorced, and the Commonwealth of Virginia essentially is saying that if you intend to be separated or divorced, then you must present yourselves as being separated in order to obtain a divorce. You cannot appear to be married while claiming to be separated.

Furthermore, when you live together with your spouse, but claim you are separated, there is a great chance for "collusion" in the eyes of the court.

Collusion is an affirmative defense to a complaint filed for divorce that essentially means that you've made up your divorce grounds.

It would be collusion if you both claimed that you were separate when you really weren't.

Finally, the public policy of the Commonwealth of Virginia is to support the family and marriage. Thus, the Commonwealth, through the legislature and the courts, is basically using the period of separation to make it *more* difficult, rather than less difficult to get divorced. As a result, some judges believe that the intent to separate is not readily manifested in an in-home separation.

## How long do we have to be separated?

In Virginia, you must be separated for either one year from the date of separation, or six months, if you meet the criteria.

The only way you can get divorced sooner (and whether it really *is* sooner is actually a debatable point – more in a moment) is if you allege and ultimately prove adultery.

## One year separation and divorce

The standard period of separation prior to finalizing an uncontested divorce is one year.

This applies whether you are moving forward with an uncontested no-fault divorce where there are minor children, or if you're finalizing on any of the fault-based grounds *except adultery.*

Cruelty? Apprehension of bodily hurt? Desertion? Abandonment? Yup – one year separation required prior to finalization.

So, if you have minor children, if you can't reach an agreement, or if you are utilizing any of the fault-based grounds for divorce except adultery, you'll have to be separated for a full year before you can finalize your divorce.

Actually, you'll have to be separated for at least 366 days, because until the 365 days have elapsed, you haven't been separated for a year. So, really, you'll have to be separated for a full year – and that's assuming that you're ready to have your agreement submitted or set your trial date on that 366th day. And I'll be honest: it would be really rare for divorce to be granted on the 366th day.

## How long will it take to get a divorce using a one-year separation?

It's impossible to say. It depends on how long it takes you to reach an agreement or, in the alternative, to fail to reach an agreement and present your case at trial.

If you reach an agreement, you have a little more flexibility. You can submit your final divorce packet to the court, if you're going the divorce by affidavit route, as soon as you have all the pieces in place. It'll usually take the court a few weeks to review your packet and grant your divorce. Sometimes more, sometimes less – but it depends on how backed up the court is.

If you don't reach an agreement and you have to set a trial, the timeline may be more out of your hands. It's hard to set a trial. Courts are often pretty backed up, and some don't have dates (especially not the hours' worth of court time you'd need to try an entire divorce case) for a pretty long time. Sometimes, it's a year or more out. It's not uncommon for courts, even courts with six or more judges on the bench, to have at least 6 months before you can set a trial date. It's not easy or quick.

And not even that, you may find that there are some procedural hoops you have to jump through – like that you have to have a judicial settlement conference before you can set a trial date. Courts have local rules that apply within their courtrooms, and you'll have to follow them – which can make your divorce take longer (and cost more money, especially if you don't settle).

All that to say, it's hard to say. It can take a long time. Or not that long, considering that you already have to be separated for a year before you can even entertain a final divorce decree being entered. And, really, a year is a fairly long time to just wait in limbo. Though we sympathize, we also don't make the rules. All we can do is help you follow them, so that you can resolve your case as quickly, inexpensively, and uneventfully as possible.

## Separation and Six-Month Divorce

There is a small contingent of cases where, because of two factors they have in common, the parties can get divorced quicker than any other couples.

**In Virginia, if you (1) don't have minor children together and (2) have already signed a separation agreement, you can get divorced after just six months of separation.**

That is the fastest you can possibly get divorced, unless you have some miracle way of *proving* adultery and scheduling a hearing faster than six months (which is unlikely).

## What does it mean to not have minor children?

It just means that those children are not 17 or younger or that you and your husband do not have minor children together. If you have a minor child from another relationship, as long as your husband did not adopt that child, you can still be divorced based on a six-month separation.

On the day that a child turns 18, he or she is no longer a child, and, therefore, not subject to a custody and/or visitation determination, and not relevant for these purposes, either.

In a lot of cases, parties don't have children – and that makes it easy. They qualify for the six-month separation automatically. But I often hear parents of grown children thinking out loud and assuming that they don't qualify because they do have children. Once your children turn 18, you qualify for the six-month separation, too.

Assuming you have a signed separation agreement.

## What's a separation agreement?

A separation agreement is a legal contract that addresses and resolves all the assets and liabilities in your marriage between you. Rather than having a judge decide, the parties agree in writing how these issues will be resolved.

If you can't reach an agreement on all issues, you go to court – and face a one-year separation.

It's ideal to be able to reach a resolution because you do the deciding. Not only that, but it often costs less, too. And it's faster! Win – win – win, right?

# GETTING THE DIVORCE STARTED: WHO SHOULD FILE FIRST?

So, you're separated. Or, at least, you understand the principles of being separated. What's next?

Well, really, it depends on the type of divorce involved. In Virginia, there are two ways to resolve your divorce: by agreement between the parties, or by a judge in court.

You can't file for divorce until you have grounds – so, in a fault-based divorce, you can file as soon as your grounds exist. In other words, the moment that he commits adultery, that he deserts the marital residence, or that he is abusive towards you. You can use his fault to file early and get into court quickly, which allows you to avail yourself of all the tools of the court. In most cases, it's a question of completing discovery or setting a date for a pendente lite hearing, which you can't do if you don't have a case filed with the court.

In a no-fault divorce, you can't file until your period of separation is up. Your grounds are based off your period of separation, so they do not exist until you've completed that one year (or six months, if you meet the criteria) of separation.

## No-fault Divorce

We've already said that, in a no-fault divorce, you can't file until your period of separation is up.

But that doesn't mean that nothing is happening between when you legally separate and once you've been separated for a year. It could mean that, but it usually doesn't.

For most people, that period of time between when they legally separate and when they file for divorce is time that they use to negotiate a signed separation agreement.

29

## What is a separation agreement?

A separation agreement is a signed contract between a husband and wife that allows them to move forward with an uncontested divorce. Instead of leaving division of assets and liabilities up to a judge, a separation agreement establishes the way the parties wish to have everything divided between them.

It's incredibly comprehensive. It includes everything – child custody, visitation, and support; spousal support; division of personal property, real property, retirement accounts, bank accounts, and investments; and more. We also include provisions about how the tax returns will be filed, what happens in the case of bankruptcy or omitted property, and exactly how transfers and divisions will take place.

We often list both separate and marital property, with the goal being that anyone who looks at the agreement can see – clearly and concisely – exactly what asset, liability, or responsibility is being described, what was supposed to happen, and within what specific time frame.

If you're dividing a bank account, for example, it's best to list the last four digits of the account number so that, if worst comes to worst and you end up in court arguing about it later, the judge can see that, yes, this is the account in question, and the division either did or didn't happen the way the agreement described.

Same with real property; you'll list the property address, classify it as marital, separate, or hybrid, and describe how it will be divided or refinanced. It should be very, very clear.

You should often even include things like separate property, even if he (or you, if it's his separate property) will benefit in no way from the disposition of the item. That way, it sets forth a specific intention to classify an item as completely separate, and outside of the jurisdiction of the divorce.

You should tread carefully with a separation agreement, too. Keep in mind that, once it's signed, it'll be very difficult – if not impossible (and, certainly, even if you *could* manage it, prohibitively expensive) – to un-sign later. If you try to do it yourself or work with a mediator to avoid hiring dedicated divorce attorneys on both sides, make sure to at least talk to an attorney beforehand to ensure that you understand your rights and entitlements under the law, and have an attorney review the proposed agreement with you before you sign.

Talking to someone who handles cases like yours day in and day out is really important, and doing a little bit of research on your own is really no substitute for getting one-on-one, Virginia-specific information directly from a divorce and custody lawyer.

## What happens once the agreement is signed?

Once the separation agreement is signed, there's very little to do (besides follow the terms of the agreement) until the period of separation is up. At that point, you can file for your uncontested divorce.

Talk to your attorney specifically about your case and what general rules you should be following, but this is often the point at which the parties move into separate living spaces, and even, in some cases, start dating again.

**An important note on dating:** Technically, you should be aware that you are married until you are divorced – not until you are separated and/or have signed a separation agreement. Adultery is a crime in Virginia and is technically punishable by law. It's probably not likely that you'd face any legal ramifications, but you could.

In an ideal world, you would wait until you were divorced before you started dating, but many people can't or won't wait that long. Ultimately, the choice (and the risk inherent with that choice) is yours.

Will it impact your spousal support? Probably not, unless your agreement says something surprising. By this point, either you were awarded spousal support, or you weren't. The whole "absolute bar" thing doesn't apply if you've already agreed to specific terms, but your spousal support may be modifiable under different circumstances. Your agreement will control, and if you have questions about this – or whether your dating before your final decree is entered could impact your entitlement to spousal support – you should talk to an attorney.

At this point, even if he has perfect proof of your adultery, he can't get a divorce using adultery as grounds (or any other fault-based grounds, for that matter). In a separation agreement, you agree to move forward with a no-fault divorce.

## What if we can't reach an agreement?

It's not always possible to reach an agreement. There may be an issue or two that is just an absolute sticking point for either or both of you.

If you aren't using fault-based grounds, you'll file on no-fault. But you'll have to wait until you've been separated for a year to do it. (You don't qualify for a divorce after a six-month separation if you aren't able to reach an agreement, so, even if you don't have minor children, you're still in the one-year camp with everyone else.)

Then, you'll have a contested divorce trial. You'll offer evidence, witnesses, and exhibits related to your proposed division of assets and liabilities, and so will he. Ultimately, a judge will decide.

## Filing for Divorce

In either case, there really isn't a strategic advantage to filing first. The party filing first is called the "plaintiff", and the person filing second is the "defendant" – but these words don't have the same meaning in a civil case as they do in a criminal case. There is no presumption against a defendant.

What's the difference? Well, a "civil" case is basically anything that is not criminal. Cases are classified in those two categories, and everything non-criminal is civil. Divorce, custody, and support are civil matters.

If you file first, you may feel like there's an advantage. At least you're not waiting for *him* to do something. And the whole experience of getting "served" is unnerving for some women to have to deal with, not to mention feeling alarmed if it also comes with a notice of a hearing. So, if you know – or highly suspect – that he's about to file, you may feel some security in the certainty of taking matters into your own hands first. But there's no actual advantage to filing first or responding to his filing, so there's no need to take preemptive action if you don't want to or aren't ready to file yet.

## Fault-Based Cases

In a fault-based case, you're automatically in court. We call these cases either "contested" cases or "litigated" cases.

Fault-based cases are more expensive than uncontested, no-fault ones, and often more expensive (though not always – since it depends entirely on the issues involved) than no-fault contested ones. Keep in mind that, in a fault-based contested case, you'll have to prove your grounds *and* argue over distribution of the assets and liabilities. In a contested no-fault case, you only argue over the distribution of the assets and liabilities.

So, why would anyone file on fault? There are actually a lot of reasons why you might file, even if it is more expensive. Here are a couple of the most common:

**1.** He cut me off
from access to any marital money.

A lot of times, people file for a fault-based contested divorce to get into court quickly and get temporary child and spousal support determined.

**2.** I don't know what assets/liabilities we have to divide.

If you haven't been responsible for bills or have very little idea what your financial assets and liabilities are, you may need to file for divorce. After you file, you'll have the opportunity to conduct discovery, which is the legal process we use to get copies of financial documents from an opposing party. We can get all sorts of information – either in written form (in interrogatories), specific copies of statements we need (in requests for production of documents), or even send subpoenas to his employer or other businesses which might have valuable information that we'd need (or that he'd try to hide).

**3.** There is an emergency custody issue that needs determining.

Custody can be determined at the juvenile court level, too, if there's no divorce pending, so it may be that your issue is better addressed there. But the circuit court – where divorces are handled – is technically a higher court, so if you file for an emergency hearing there and then he files for divorce, it'll be divested and go up to circuit court anyway.

It's worth discussing your options with an attorney to see where you should file, but if you're going to get divorced anyway your issue may be better heard in circuit court. And if there's an emergency, you may want to file right away!

**4.** He refuses to sign anything at all, or we just can't reach an agreement.

There are a lot of different shades to this fourth reason. Maybe he says he doesn't care what you send him, he won't sign anything ever. Maybe you just can't agree on how to divide something, or whether support should be awarded, or how custody and visitation will be shared.

If you just can't agree, you just can't agree. And there's no special legal voodoo we can do to make him agreeable if he's just … not. If you can't agree, you go to court, and that's all there is to it.

## I have to file on fault, but I don't want to go to trial. Will I have another option, later on, if we can reach an agreement eventually?

Yes, of course! Your case may look contested right now, and you may even file on fault. But even though the train is on the tracks, that doesn't mean you can't change course.

At any point, you can go from a fault to a no-fault case. Just because you file on fault doesn't mean you're stuck. We can negotiate an agreement and attempt to resolve the entire case at any point.

On the other side, if you thought you could negotiate an agreement but just can't get him to budge, you can still either file on fault grounds (if you have them and want to use them) or, in the alternative, no-fault grounds. There's a lot of flexibility.

### The Pendente Lite Hearing

Pendente lite is Latin for "while the litigation is pending".

In a divorce case, Pendente Lite (pronounced pen-deet-tay light-tay, or PL, for short) is often the first opportunity to get in front of a judge.

The party who files for a pendent lite hearing first, is usually the person who gets to talk first. This is an opportunity to establish a couple of key points, including but not limited to temporary child and spousal support, the issuance of certain restraining orders and injunctions (like, against harassment of the other party or of wasting or disposing of marital assets), exclusive possession of the marital residence, custody and visitation, and advancing of attorney's fees from the other party.

We often encourage clients to file first if they want temporary (*Pendente Lite*) relief. The reason for filing first is both strategic and tactical.

Doing so is **STRATEGIC** because oftentimes husbands need a legal wake-up call to show that he is not in control anymore and to also let him know that you are leveling the playing field with your new lawyer.

Doing so is **TACTICAL** because when you file your Complaint for Divorce, you are also going to have him served a notice and motion for temporary (*Pendente Lite*) relief. When you file this *Pendente Lite* Motion first, you get to speak first. This means your lawyer, representing you, the "moving party", gets first dibs on influencing the judge with your view of the facts.

At the conclusion of the temporary support and custody hearing, your lawyer speaks, then your husband's lawyer speaks and then often your lawyer gets the benefit of the last word. While the last word is not always permitted in temporary hearings, it is always permitted in the final custody or divorce hearings, and it is a valuable right; the right of being the last to be heard when trying to influence the judge.

# LET THE DIVORCE BEGIN: WHAT DOES THE PROCESS ACTUALLY ENTAIL?

Divorces can take a few different forms, depending on what choices you make at the outset of the process.

If you're trying to negotiate an agreement outside of court, there aren't specific steps to follow. You can negotiate entirely back and forth through email or physical letters, or you can participate in a 4 way or settlement conference, or mediation.

In a contested divorce, on the other hand, you'll have to follow the court rules and procedures to move your case forward.

A divorce starts – as far as the court is concerned – when a complaint is filed.

## Complaint

The Complaint is the formal legal document that opens up a case with the court. In it, you allege the facts and establish the statutory requirements for the divorce - the date of marriage, date of separation, names and dates of birth of children, marriage location, where the parties lived at the time of the separation, and whether fault or no-fault grounds exist with regards to the divorce.

If your grounds are no-fault-based, you'll say so – so your date of separation should be one year, or six months if you meet the criteria, prior to the date you filed.

If your grounds are fault-based, you'll make your allegations, too. At this point, you don't need to prove that your grounds exist, but you will need to demonstrate that you have a reasonable belief that what you allege is true.

36

In the case of an adultery allegation, for example, you might want to allege the name or initials of the other woman, if you know, or any facts or circumstances that you're aware of that support your allegation.

These documents can get pretty nasty. Of course, they can also be pretty matter of fact, too, especially in an uncontested, no-fault divorce where an agreement between the parties has already resolved all of the outstanding issues and all that's left is for a divorce decree to be entered. But if your divorce is contested, you should be prepared to read some things in the complaint, if he files first, that make you uncomfortable or upset.

You will normally sign the complaint under oath, because all the allegations you make are under penalty of perjury.

If yours include no-fault grounds, your attorney could sign the complaint on your behalf, but depending on the specific allegations contained therein, she may not be comfortable doing so. To sign a complaint means that you are essentially verifying the veracity of the terms contained in it, so your attorney may not want to sign it. (After all, we usually can't even actually verify with any certainty exactly what the date of separation is – we didn't live there with you and witness it!)

You are now known as the "Plaintiff." The Complaint is then filed in the circuit court for the city where you last lived as husband and wife, or alternatively, where your husband, now known as the "Defendant," currently resides.

After processing the Complaint, the Clerk of the Circuit Court will either forward it to the Sheriff's Office for service, or your attorney may hire a private process server who will serve the Complaint on your husband. The current cost of filing a divorce in Virginia Beach in 2021 is $84.00 and the cost of service by the Sheriff's Office is $12.00, whereas the cost of service by a private process server will normally be between $25.00 and $50.00. The cost of private process service can be much higher if there are difficulties in serving your husband. The actual divorce doesn't really start until your husband is served with the Complaint, and you have up to one year after filing the Complaint to complete service.

Within twenty-one days following the service of the Complaint on your husband, he will normally file an Answer and often a Counterclaim. (And, likewise, if he happens to have filed the

Complaint first, you'll have an opportunity to respond, within 21 days, with your own Answer and Counterclaim.)

An Answer and Counterclaim is the opposing party's opportunity to respond to the allegations that were made against them, as well as to issue their own set of allegations.

Whether he files first or responds with his own Answer and Counterclaim, if your case is contested you should prepare yourself to read things that make you angry, indignant, or scared.

It is not uncommon for answers or cross-complaints to have exaggerated allegations against you. More often than not, the allegations are designed to disturb you or intimidate you. Moreover, sometimes the allegations as written by your husband's attorney are as much to show his or her own client his lawyer is "tough" than it is about your actual conduct. Remember, the attorney is creatively writing what he or she was told and is trying to make it as negative as possible about you. Don't let it push your buttons; stay calm. Remember, do the unexpected, and do not let him shake you.

If issues of temporary support need to be immediately addressed, then a *Pendente Lite* hearing is scheduled, where the court will rule on temporary spousal and child support, temporary custody and visitation, hospitalization insurance and restraining orders regarding possession of the home, no harassment, no wasting of assets and if minor children are involved, no unrelated overnight guests of the opposite sex. Once these issues are addressed and ruled upon by the court, then the longer-term issues regarding your divorce can be addressed during the time remaining before your Final Divorce.

## What if what he alleges about me isn't true??

Like we said, allegations are often exaggerated! Sometimes, they're blatantly untrue.

Ultimately, nothing matters until you have proven your grounds exist to the satisfaction of the judge, so you really shouldn't worry about allegations yet. If anything, you should be thinking about how to begin to plan the case to your advantage – because, in many cases, getting into court early IS an advantage!

It's not like he can just allege anything he wants, though – there are standards, after all. You also have some options available to you. If he files first, your answer and counterclaim can include your specific response to his allegations, in as much detail as you (and your lawyer) like. If his allegations are contained in his answer and counterclaim, you can also file an answer to the counterclaim, where you respond specifically to his allegations.

In many cases, attorneys don't like to go into too much detail too early on, but it's still an opportunity for you to lay the groundwork for what you'll ultimately prove at trial. If what he's alleged is blatantly and obviously untrue, you may have a lot of evidence you can use to prove your innocence! That'll be helpful, and now is definitely a good time to begin to work with your attorney on a strategy and gather the evidence you need to disprove his allegations.

Additionally, if what he has alleged is untrue, or if certain specific circumstances exist, you can plead an affirmative defense.

## Affirmative Defenses

An affirmative defense means that you're essentially saying, "Yes, it's true, but there are extenuating circumstances that you should know about!"

The five defenses are as follows:

### 1. Condonation

When you resume cohabitation *after* learning of the conduct that constitutes the grounds for divorce, you have condoned it.

You have condoned his adultery if you have sex with him *after* you find out about it! To preserve adultery as your grounds for divorce, you should not have sex with him after you find out.

You do not forgive adultery that you don't know about – or simply suspect. You also don't forgive subsequent acts of adultery, with the same or with a different partner, if you have no knowledge of it. But, at some point, proving what was known, when, and how becomes complicated, so keep that in mind, too.

This applies to the other fault-based grounds as well. If he deserts or abandons you, and then you let him back into the home, you've condoned the earlier desertion or abandonment.

### 2. Insanity

When the party at fault is insane.

In order to be at fault, your husband has to have the mental capacity to understand his actions.

This one's easy: if you've alleged grounds against him, his defense could be that he's too affected by mental illness to understand the nature of his actions.

Of course, he'd have to prove his mental illness – or you would, if the shoe were on the other foot.

### 3. Collusion:

When the parties make up a false ground for divorce.

You can't just say, "Oh, let's allege adultery, and get it over more quickly!" Well, you can, but it's perjury – and your husband could ultimately slap you with collusion when you use those grounds to file for divorce.

Ultimately this doesn't really even make sense anymore; an uncontested, no-fault divorce is often quicker and easier than any fault-based, contested divorce, so it doesn't really even happen. But, if it did, this affirmative defense would apply if the other spouse ultimately didn't feel comfortable perjuring himself or herself in court.

### 4. Recrimination:

Recrimination basically means that you can't BOTH commit the same fault-based grounds for divorce, and then use them against each other.

In a case where this happens, the two faults cancel each other out.

A good example? When both spouses commit adultery. In such a case, the court does not grant a divorce on the grounds of adultery.

### 5. Connivance:

Connivance means that you can't set your spouse up by appearing to agree to the situation, and then turn around and use it against them in the divorce.

For instance, a wife cannot set up husband with a prostitute and then file divorce on adultery after he has sex with her.

## An important note on affirmative defenses

It's important to note that an affirmative defense – or the use of one – does not mean that the parties will have to stay married. It's just a defense against the grounds used to achieve the divorce.

In any case, you still have the option to use no-fault grounds for divorce (so, based just on your period of separation).

There is really nothing in the law that will force an unwilling spouse to stay married. The divorce doesn't just go away or get dismissed because a defense is employed.

## What if I don't want a divorce?

We come across situations all the time where the parties are not on the same page about the divorce. It's a really difficult situation to find yourself in, no matter which side you fall on.

Still, it's important to know that there's ultimately really nothing either of you can do to stop the process entirely. You can slow it down and make it more expensive – but you can't stop it.

It's always wise to consider your objectives. What do you hope to accomplish? And – at what price?

Whether it's you or he who is holding on to the marriage, it's wise for you to work with a licensed Virginia divorce and custody attorney so that you can make sure to respond in a way that keeps your best interests in mind. Even if you'd prefer to stay, you'll likely find that your bottom line is better suited by going along with the divorce. Likewise, if he's the one holding on, you'll find that using an attorney to help you strong arm the case forward will likely help you save both time and money.

# HOW YOU OBTAIN INFORMATION AFTER A DIVORCE IS FILED: THE DISCOVERY PROCESS

Once the complaint and the answer and counterclaim have been received by the court, the case begins in earnest. You may have a Pendente Lite hearing, like we've already discussed, but you'll also have an opportunity (and so will he) to conduct formal discovery.

This is where you start to gather the information about the case that you'll need to prepare for trial.

### What if my divorce is uncontested?

Discovery – at least, formal discovery – is only conducted in contested cases.

In separation agreement cases, there is not discovery. There may be some exchange of information between the sides; in fact, in most cases, there is. But it's not formal discovery, and there's no ability to force the other side to provide the required information.

One of the reasons you might consider filing a contested divorce, especially if you don't have all the financial information you might need to draft a comprehensive separation agreement, is to conduct formal discovery through the court.

If your husband is not willing to share documents, if there's not transparency, or if you are uninformed about the assets and liabilities, you may want to consider filing for divorce.

### What is discovery?

Discovery is a broad name we use to apply to the process of figuring out what the issues are in a case. We use the same word in different kinds of cases – like personal injury, for example – but what, exactly, we are looking for will be different in a divorce or custody case.

In a divorce case, we're often looking most closely at the financial documents. In a custody case, we may be looking for medical records, for criminal convictions, or other information that might help us to prove that whatever dad wants in the way of custody is not going to be in the child's best interests.

In other words, the discovery process is highly specific to each unique case.

There are a number of different ways we can go about getting that information.

## Interrogatories

Interrogatories are a set of questions – in Virginia, you're allowed no more than thirty – that the responding party has to answer. It's done in a simple question an answer format.

The specific questions used will speak to the theory of the case or the issues presented, but generally include questions on assets owned, debts owed, why he thinks he should have custody, and so on. It's also common to ask for the names of any witnesses or experts or exhibits intended by the opposing party for use at trial. (It's only in movies where these things are a surprise!)

These questions go into great detail about your assets, liabilities, fault, custody and such other issues as may be raised in the divorce. Just to give you an idea, here's a couple sample questions you might see in a typical set of interrogatories:

**1.** Provide the following information as to each employment position you have held during the past five years, whether full- time, part-time, or self-employment, free-lance or contract work, including but not limited to, your employer's name, the name of your immediate supervisor, each employer's full address and telephone number, your position, your dates of service, your hours worked, your current monthly and annual gross income, listing each source separately (including bonuses, commissions, tips and overtime, stock options, deferred compensation for each year) and your fringe benefits (including insurance, retirement, profit sharing, travel pay, vacation and sick leave accrued), and state the reasons for any changes in employment and for your current employment state how often you are paid (i.e. monthly, every two weeks) and state the date when you are next paid.

**2.** Provide the following information as to all bank accounts, in your name individually, jointly with any other person or in the name of any entity (i.e. partnership, corporation or otherwise) in which you have an interest, or that is held on your behalf, in any banking institutions, savings and loans, credit unions, stock brokerage firms, or other financial or financially related corporations, from January 1, 2020 to the date of your answers, stating the name, address and telephone number of the institution, each account number(s) and the type of account, owner(s) and signatories on each account, the balance of each account as of the date of separation, as well as the present balance(s) of the accounts.

**3.** Provide the following information as to all Individual Retirement Accounts (IRA), Simplified Employee Pension Plans (SEP), Keogh Plans, profit-sharing, 401k plans, 403(B) plans, thrift savings plans, stock plans, retirement or pension plans, deferred compensation plans, defined contribution plans, defined benefits plan and annuities to which you are or may be entitled to receive benefits. State the name of the institution, where the funds are maintained, the business address and phone number of the institutional custodian of the funds, the name and account number of each account, the balance of each account as of separation, present balance, and whether you claim the funds are marital, separate, or hybrid.

**4.** If you believe that your spouse is not fit to have custody of or visitation with the child of the marriage, then state in detail what you allege to be the factors and circumstances which bring you to that conclusion including specific facts, actions, dates of occurrence, the persons involved and the persons witnessing such events.

**5.** Identify every person who has knowledge of the issues pending in this case, whether on the issue of the grounds of divorce, or on any financial issues such as custody, child support, spousal support or equitable distribution, stating their current address and their home and work phone numbers, their relationship to the parties involved; if the person will be called as an expert witness, state their name, address, telephone number, and profession, and set forth the subject matter on which the expert is expected to testify, the opinion they will express and a summary of the grounds for each opinion.

## Request for Production of Documents

Interrogatories get you answers to specific questions in a narrative form. But where's the proof?

In addition to interrogatories, you're also permitted to ask for specific documents in your husband's possession or documents he has ready access to. This is called a "motion for production of documents.

In many cases, interrogatories and requests for production of documents are submitted together, and the questions more or less mirror each other through the documents. Unlike interrogatories, though, there is no limit the number of RPDs.

If you need statements about his retirement accounts, his credit card debt, bank accounts, pay stubs, LES statements, or other documentation, this is likely the place to get it.

Again, here are a couple sample requests for production that you might see:

*Please Provide:*

1. All pay statements, or any other proof of income from any source, whether received from employers or from any entity in which you have an interest, reflecting gross income (whether taxable or non-taxable) and gains (realized or unrealized) and all withholdings, as well as income for overtime work, commissions, tips, bonuses, and all contracts and/or correspondence evidencing any terms or conditions of employment, that were in effect or were entered into, from January 1, 2020 to the present.

2. All savings, checking, depository, investment or loan account statements, checks, and registers, reflecting deposits, withdrawals, and account balances in any banking institutions, savings and loan association, credit union, brokerage accounts or accounts with other financial institutions or corporations, partnerships or businesses, whether such account has been held by you individually, jointly with any other person, or in the name of any entity in which you have an interest, or that is held on your behalf, from January 1, 2020 to the present.

3. All summary plan descriptions and/or statements for each pension or retirement benefits plan, expense account, cafeteria plan, profit-sharing, stock option plan, 401k plan, 403(b) plan, thrift savings plan, deferred compensation plan, IRA, Keogh, SEP,

or other retirement or pension plan, vested or non-vested, as well as any military pension plans, either by reason of employment with another or from any entity in which you have an interest from January 1, 2020 to the present.

4. All reports of any experts that you intend to call to testify at trial.

5. Any and all tangible evidence, including documents, correspondence, letters, video and/or audio tape recordings, photographs or prepared exhibits which prove, support or are relevant to your petition for custody.

## Subpoena Duces Tecum

A Subpoena Duces Tecum is a specific type of subpoena requesting supporting documentation. It can be sent directly to a third party – like an employer or a bank.

You see, technically speaking, a party must only provide information that is in his "possession or control" so, sometimes, games are played.

If he's saying he doesn't have the documents or can't provide them, you may find it cheaper, easier, and more efficient to get it directly from the source.

For example, we can send a Subpoena Duces Tecum to your husband's employer requesting documents that will provide information about his benefits and retirement as well as copies of his last twelve months' pay records.

Sometimes, we also have to use a Subpoena Duces Tecum (or SDT) to get information that he'd prefer to keep quiet – like, perhaps, records relating to his termination. If he has, for example, a hidden bank account, we can sometimes employ a SDT to get to that information as well. We've even seen a SDT used to uncover adultery – by requesting phone, hotel, or credit card information that wasn't turned over earlier in discovery!

While having to send a Subpoena Duces Tecum is an added expense, quite frequently it is very helpful in putting together accurate financial information.

## Requests for Admissions

Another effective weapon in the discovery arsenal is a Request for Admissions. Admissions are very fact-specific and *must* be answered within 21 days.

Most of the time admissions are used to verify documents or other specific facts needed to prove the theory of the case. Some Admissions examples follow:

1. Admit or deny that your total gross income for the year 2020 is $67,290.00.
2. Admit or deny that you had a checking account at Bank of America with Ms. Feckless during the month of March of 2020.
3. Admit or deny that you have contributed to a 401K Plan with your current employer during the calendar year 2020.

**Important Note about Requests for Admissions:** If you are ever served admissions, you MUST respond! The deadline here is very strict. If you fail to admit or deny an allegation, the allegation will be deemed admitted for the purposes of your litigation.

That means that, regardless of whether it's true or not, the requests for admissions will be construed against you in an unfavorable light – which can be really damning in your case! Do *not* miss the deadline!

## Depositions

In a deposition, both parties appear with their attorneys and a court reporter. Usually, only one party's – or witness's- deposition is taken on a given day.

It's a lot like being questioned on the witness stand at trial. The court reporter takes down the responses verbatim, and you (or whoever is being deposed) is sworn under oath and is under penalty of perjury.

It's not commonly used in a divorce case, but, when it is, is often utilized to great effect for a specific purpose. A good example would be deposing a girlfriend about her adulterous relationship with a husband or questioning a party in detail about their sources of income and debts (especially in a case that is unusually complicated).

Depositions allow your attorney to ask your husband questions to gather further information and to lock in his testimony. Depositions are under oath and may be admitted as evidence in a court hearing if the underlying questions are admissible. Depositions may also be taken of third parties such as girlfriends, babysitters, teachers, or other persons who may have information important to your case. Frequently, successful depositions can expedite settlement.

## Motion to Compel

You can send discovery all you want, but what happens if your husband does not respond?

Once a case is filed with the court, you have the ability to use the power and influence of the court to get things done.

One of the things that the court can help you with is ensuring that discovery is answered.

Your attorney can file a motion to compel, which essentially asks the court to order him to answer the questions presented.

Ultimately, if he's ordered to provide the information and again does not, he could ultimately find himself facing a contempt hearing, find that certain evidence at trial is inadmissible, or even have attorney's fees awarded to you.

**A note on attorney's fees:** We do, sometimes, see attorney's fees awarded in cases like this, where a party was supposed to do something but did not (especially if they were ordered to do it by the court and *still* did not respond, or did not respond fully and satisfactorily).

You will almost certainly not get *all* of your attorney's fees, though; that almost never happens. The courts usually express the opinion that both parties are responsible for hiring attorneys that they can afford.

*But,* in a situation like this, you may find that the court makes him responsible for the fees you expended in your various motions to compel, or whatever other actions you had to take to make him comply with what the court requires of him anyway. It's a limited award of fees, but it does help keep people honest and prevent you from being penalized for making sure he follows the rules.

## Options to resolve your divorce case

After all the discovery information is obtained, you have a choice about how to proceed. Either you negotiate a signed separation agreement, or you litigate.

Now that you've gone through discovery, all the necessary disclosures have been made, you've had a chance to get temporary support established, and you've gotten a few bills from your attorney, you may be in a better position to settle than you were before.

After all, it's either that – or you let the judge decide how all of your assets and liabilities will be divided, and how custody will be shared between the two of you.

It's also not as though, at this point, you can just schedule a trial for next week and get the thing done. In fact, in many courts, it's not unusual to have to wait a year to get a date set for a full divorce and/or custody trial. So, whether you're able to reach an agreement now or not, chances are pretty good you'll have some time to think about it.

## Separation Agreement

What is a separation agreement?

Earlier in the book, we discussed that a separation agreement is a legal contract that records how you and your soon-to-be ex have agreed to divide all the assets, liabilities, and responsibilities between you.

Ultimately, 90 to 95 percent of all divorces ultimately conclude with a separation agreement; however, how you arrive at an agreement is often a convoluted process. The separation agreement is often the result of negotiations or mediation. .

Don't make the mistake of thinking that people who reach an agreement do so easily, because, though that can sometimes be the case, it isn't always so.

In describing these resolution options, I have purposely left out the collaborative divorce model, as that will be covered in a separate section. The reason collaboration is not included is that one does not normally file a divorce complaint in a collaborative case, but rather, one agrees not to go to court and not to file a divorce suit until the matter is totally resolved with a written agreement.

## Negotiation

Turning to the option of negotiation of a separation agreement, it is common that negotiations commence with one side providing the other side a written offer of the terms by which they would settle the divorce. Then the other side responds with their terms of settlement. From here, the parties continue to give and take until all of the issues of the family are resolved.

Remember, in negotiations, ultimatums are not looked upon favorably, as they make settlement of issues very difficult, if not impossible.

If the parties are able to resolve matters through negotiations, then the end product will be a separation agreement which outlines all the terms of settlement. This document will then become the final terms of your divorce.

This brings to mind a *cardinal rule* that during a divorce a woman should never sign any documents without first having them reviewed by her attorney. Frequently, I have had women come to see me with an agreement they signed saying, "Oh, my husband told me this was just a temporary agreement" when, in fact, the document states right on the face of it that this is a final stipulation agreement. We liken a Separation agreement to your Bill of Rights, your Constitution, and your Declaration of Independence all rolled up in one document!

It is very important that you not sign any such document until your attorney has reviewed it with you! Whatever the advantages and disadvantages of your particular agreement, you should not sign until you know, understand, and agree to them. We cannot stress how many times women have brought signed agreements to me thinking that they could change the terms at a later time.

There is nothing worse than having to tell a woman that what she's signed can't be unsigned, or that she's given away her entitlement to something that would have made a tremendous difference to her post-divorce. We really can't stress to you enough how important this is for your financial future.

The courts of the Commonwealth of Virginia do not often set aside contracts, and the fact that a wife was emotionally depressed and/or incapable of saying "no" to her husband is seldom, if ever, sufficient grounds to legally undo a signed written agreement.

## Things you should know about Separation Agreements

**First** - We like to say that the only limitations in a separation agreement is your own creativity! Whatever solution you and your husband can agree to, your agreement can be drafted to reflect.

The judge won't be able to approach your case this way; he or she will use certain, narrow, specific provisions that can apply with relative fairness across the board. It's only when you negotiate a separation agreement that you truly have the freedom to craft a solution that works for you, your ex, and your children post-divorce.

**Second** - A separation agreement is a legally binding and enforceable contract between you and your husband. *Do not write and sign your own separation agreement without having it reviewed by an experienced divorce attorney looking out solely for your legal interests.*
**<u>YOUR HUSBAND'S ATTORNEY CANNOT REPRESENT YOU!</u>**

**Third** – Custody, Visitation and Child Support are *always subject to change based on a material change of circumstance*, so don't give away support or assets to obtain custody of your children. I have seen cases where the woman gave up financial assets for custody, only to lose custody several years later because her finances were unstable, while her former spouse was prospering financially. The pre-teen and teen kids wanted to live at the house with the pool, the big allowance, the ski vacations and the 4-wheeler and the *Guardian Ad Litem* (an attorney often appointed by the court to represent the child) disapproved of mom taking the youngest to work with her because she could not afford daycare. Do not let such a scenario happen to you.

In short, if you give up everything to obtain custody, you may well lose custody several years later, primarily because you gave up everything!

**Fourth** - In your agreement, make sure you include times and dates when things are going to be completed. Time is of the essence may be the most important five words you use with regard to financial payments.

**Fifth** - Details are very important and add clarity. Be careful of broad strokes! Vagueness may create huge misunderstandings which can be exploited by your ex and expensive to resolve.

## Mediation

A second method of resolving the terms of a divorce is mediation.

Mediation is a process where you and your husband meet with a mediator to discuss and attempt to resolve the issues of your divorce.

Mediators are not usually attorneys. Even if a mediator IS an attorney, though, you have to remember that he or she has not been hired to represent you. A mediator's only job is to help you reach an agreement, not to give you advice, tell you what a judge might order, or educate you on your rights and entitlements under the law.

If the parties agree, they may bring their attorneys to their mediation sessions, but that's not common. Most of the time, people use mediators in an attempt to avoid using attorneys – with mixed results.

My advice to women who choose the mediation process is to meet with their attorney in advance and develop an outline of the issues and an acceptable range of terms of agreement with regard to each issue.

Going into mediation unprepared can be very costly, especially if you have no idea what your rights and entitlements are!

Additionally, it's also smart to meet with your attorney again *after* mediation to review the agreement that the mediator has prepared. Remember: a mediator is usually not an attorney!

An attorney's job when drafting an agreement is to do two things: (1) to memorialize the proposed or agreed upon terms in the most favorable way to our client, and (2) to minimize future problems. A mediator isn't so concerned about future problems; he or she hasn't spent her career litigating over bad agreements! We've seen some terrible agreements, and we've seen people spend tens of thousands of dollars arguing over what they were meant to mean or attempting to correct them. Our agreements are specifically designed to help avoid the problems we've seen – saving you money in the long run.

Mediation can be a great option, but it isn't a good fit for everyone. If you're intimidated by your spouse or if he has a history of forcing you to bend to his will, mediation (or, at least, mediation without an attorney present) may not be the best option for you.

## Litigation

Litigation means going to court and letting the judge decide.

There are a number of reasons people might find themselves in court, even if they wish they didn't have to be. For one thing, if your husband refuses to negotiate with you, you'll have no choice. After all, the assets, liabilities, and responsibilities arising from the marriage *will* be addressed – either by the two of you or by the judge -before your divorce can be granted. If an issue, asset or debt is not raised at trial, it is waived forever.

Also, if you don't know the assets and liabilities, you may want to file for a divorce so that you can go through the discovery process. It's too difficult to write an agreement without all the pieces to the puzzle (and you risk losing valuable assets on the table just because you didn't know), so filing may be the right path.

If he's not reasonable, too, you may find that you have to file. A dispute over spousal support, for example, or his stubborn refusal to give you your share of the retirement is probably a good reason to file a divorce.

In general, though, litigated divorces are among the most expensive and most time consuming. They also give the parties the least control over how their assets and liabilities will ultimately be divided, which isn't ideal. (People who negotiate and resolve their own divorces indicate the greatest degree of satisfaction with both the results and the process.)

If you find yourself in court in your divorce case, you will have a trial before a judge (there is no jury) where evidence will be presented on your behalf and on behalf of your husband.

The judge will ultimately make decisions regarding each and every issue presented to him or her, and the final decree of divorce will be entered based on the judge's decision.

The most important thing about litigation is to make sure that you and your attorney are fully prepared for the process.

There are many strict deadlines for providing information to each of the parties and to the court which, if not followed, can be disastrous to your case. Accordingly, if you anticipate litigation, then you will need to be able to provide the time to become adequately prepared.

## Appeal

What if the court rules wrongly?

After your trial, the attorneys will draft a final decree of divorce based on the Court's decision, and it will be entered by the court.

You will then have thirty days from the date of the entry of that order to note an appeal if you disagree with the Judge's ruling. While appealing a divorce is a matter of right, meaning you don't need the Judge to make a mistake, the number of cases Court of Appeals reverses is extremely low. The appeals court give a significant amount of discretion to the trial judge. Most importantly, it is not uncommon for the Court of Appeals to award attorney's fees to the non-appealing party if the Court believes the appeal is frivolous. Because of this, most cases are not appealed.

The appellate process in Virginia usually takes between six months and a year and can be quite costly. It's definitely best to discuss your options for an appeal with your attorney

## Collaboration

The collaborative divorce process permits couples to work through issues involving their children, their financial future and their property using joint problem-solving techniques *without going to court or threatening to go to court.*

With the help of supportive professionals serving in the capacity of coaches, child specialists and financial specialists, the clients, their attorneys, and all the other professionals, work together to achieve an agreement that addresses the interests and priorities of both spouses as well as the family as a whole.

For that reason, collaborative divorce has very high success rate.

Collaborative divorce isn't just something you stumble across; it's a deliberate choice that both you and your husband have to make. You'll choose and specifically hire collaboratively trained attorneys, make a pledge not to go to court, and hire a team or professionals to help you in the decision-making process.

It's definitely a worthwhile process, but one that you'll need to deliberately seek out.

## Spousal Support

Spousal support is one of the more challenging areas of law. Unlike child support, which governed almost exclusively by the formula, spousal support awards can vary dramatically.

Ultimately, the first question is whether or not you'll receive spousal support at all – it's never a guarantee.

There are three criteria which govern whether or not you will receive support.

**1.** Need v. Ability to Pay

It's quite easy to demonstrate that you have a need. In most cases, we use an income and expense sheet to show what your monthly expenses are, and to demonstrate that you don't have enough money coming in to meet your very reasonable needs. Of course, it won't be enough to say that you need $1000 a month for groceries for yourself; there will be some scrutiny applied to the numbers you provide. But we can take an in-depth look at your expenses and the money that you have coming in to meet them in order to fulfill the first prong of this test.

Ability to pay, on the other hand, is a little trickier. An ability to pay means that he earns significantly more than you. If he earns less, about the same, or only slightly more than you, you will not receive spousal support. In general, he must earn a LOT more than you do – usually, 40-50% or more beyond what you earn.

If you can't show both things – that you have a need, and he has an ability to pay – you won't receive support at all.

**2.** The statutory factors

The Virginia Code also sets forth some standards when it comes to spousal support.

Whether your case is litigated (meaning that we're fighting over spousal support in court) or negotiated, the bulk of your attorney's argument for why you deserve to receive support should be supported by these factors:

- The obligations, needs and financial resources of the parties, including but not limited to income from all pension, profit sharing or retirement plans, of whatever nature;
- The standard of living established during the marriage;
- The duration of the marriage;
- The age and physical and mental condition of the parties and any special circumstances of the family;
- The extent to which the age, physical or mental condition or special circumstances of any child of the parties would make it appropriate that a party not seek employment outside of the home;
- The contributions, monetary and nonmonetary, of each party to the well-being of the family;
- The property interests of the parties, both real and personal, tangible and intangible;
- The provisions made with regard to the marital property under § 20-107.3;
- The earning capacity, including the skills, education and training of the parties and the present employment opportunities for persons possessing such earning capacity;
- The opportunity for, ability of, and the time and costs involved for a party to acquire the appropriate education, training and employment to obtain the skills needed to enhance his or her earning ability;
- The decisions regarding employment, career, economics, education and parenting arrangements made by the parties during the marriage and their effect on present and future

earning potential, including the length of time one or both of the parties have been absent from the job market;

- The extent to which either party has contributed to the attainment of education, training, career position or profession of the other party; and

- Such other factors, including the tax consequences to each party and the circumstances and factors that contributed to the dissolution, specifically including any ground for divorce, as are necessary to consider the equities between the parties.

**3.   The duration of marriage**

When it comes to spousal support, there are really three questions: (1) whether spousal support will be awarded at all, (2) then, if so, how much, and (3) then, if so, for how long?

All three of these factors relate to the first question. How much you'll receive will ultimately come down to the first prong of the test (need versus ability to pay – and how much more he earns than you).

The third prong relates, of course, to whether you'll receive support at all, but, also, to the question of *how long* you'll receive support.

If you read the statute, you'll see no mention of how long you must be married to receive support, or any hard and fast rules regarding how long awards of support are ordered. Still, it matters!

Many years ago, there was a proposed law that would have specifically codified how long you had to be married to receive support. It didn't pass, but there is still a sort of preconceived notion that, the longer your marriage, the longer your award of support.

Again – there's not a formal rule, so a lot of this is established by convention and a long standard of having done things a certain way. The factors and other circumstances related to your marriage will ultimately play into your award of spousal support, too, so keep in mind that there is a fair amount of lawyering that often goes into these awards as well.

Still, we have these preconceived notions, and they tell us a few things. First, that short term marriages of 1-7 or so years, that spousal support should not be awarded. For marriages between 7-8 and 17-19 years or so, that support should be awarded (again, assuming that support would otherwise be awarded – it's not an automatic entitlement based solely on the length of your marriage) for half the length of the marriage. In long term marriages, on the other hand, permanent spousal support becomes a possibility.

## A Note on Permanent Spousal Support

Permanent spousal support isn't forever and ever, no matter what happens! Spousal support terminates – even permanent spousal support – on death, remarriage, or cohabitation with someone analogous to marriage for twelve consecutive months.

That's established specifically by statute, and there's nothing we can do about it. You'll likely see this language in your agreement; maybe not in your court order, but the rules still apply. It's the statute, after all.

What does that mean, though? Death, remarriage, or cohabitation?

If either of you dies, spousal support will terminate.

If the recipient spouse remarries, spousal support will terminate.

If the recipient spouse cohabitates in a relationship analogous to marriage for a period of *one year or more*, spousal support will terminate.

## What is a "relationship analogous to marriage"?

A relationship analogous to marriage is a tricky thing. Basically, it means that you live with someone, and you derive your support from him or her.

It does not necessarily mean that you're in a romantic relationship. In fact, I've heard of at least one case where spousal support was terminated when two single moms lived together with their children, shared expenses and childcare responsibilities between them, with absolutely no romantic relationship whatsoever.

There's a difference, legally, between a roommate – where you just share a home, but don't actively help each other – and someone that you lean on for financial support, like a spouse.

That's not the typical scenario, of course, and the actual termination part would be super fact specific and likely subject to a judge's ruling (because who would voluntarily agree to let their spousal support award terminate?). Most of the time, a 'relationship analogous to marriage' is a romantic relationship, like a live-in boyfriend.

You could solve this problem by maintaining your own separate residences, and even if you do have adult sleepovers, not living together full time until after your spousal support award terminates.

## How is spousal support paid in Virginia?

Most of the time, spousal support is paid monthly, but, technically, there are four types of spousal support awards available in divorce.

The courts are empowered to award any one type of support or any combination of types of support it deems appropriate.

The types of support are lump sum award, periodic payments, rehabilitative support for a fixed period of time, and reservation of right to ask for support at a future time.

## Lump Sum Spousal Support

It's not usual, but it happens occasionally that, rather than make monthly payments, spousal support is paid in one lump sum.

It's actually a really interesting take on spousal support. In most cases, the resources just aren't actually there to pay spousal support in this way.

If you *do* get spousal support paid in one lump sum, though, your award wouldn't be subject to the terminating factors. Since it's already paid before you die, remarry, or cohabit, these conditions no longer apply – freeing you up to pursue your post-divorce life on your own terms.

It would free him, in a way, too, in the sense that he wouldn't have to make a monthly payment for a longer period of time. A cleaner break.

Determining how much support you should receive in a lump sum payment is usually the subject of some pretty intense negotiations. You can run guidelines (they exist, even if they're not binding except on a temporary basis in a case where the parties earn less than $10,000 combined monthly), multiply by a certain number of years, add in when you predict that he'll retire – and at least begin negotiations. But I imagine that you'll both have to make some compromises here – after all, there's a cost to him from coming up with this money up front, and a benefit to you to have it all at once, rather than having to wait for it.

There are no hard and fast rules; there's only what you can agree to in negotiations, and what you can't. It's probably pretty unlikely that lump sum support would be awarded by a judge. This is more likely something that would be the result of negotiations between the parties.

## Periodic Payments of Spousal Support

The most common spousal support arrangement is periodic payments, which means that you'll receive a certain amount of money per week for a specified period of time.

Periodic spousal support can be for any period of time, say, for example, five or ten years (or even defined by the exact number of months), but it can also be "permanent", which means that there's no specific termination date (but it could, depending on the award, still be modifiable).

## Rehabilitative Support

Rehabilitative support is technically spousal support designed to get a payee spouse back on her feet. It may be designed to last for a specific period of time designed to help the payee spouse go back to school to get a degree (allowing her to earn a higher income), or to last until she has a change to renew a trade license or certification necessary to work in her field.

Sometimes, it's awarded like periodic support – as in, an amount of money paid each month for a specific term – or it could also be staggered so that the spouse receives a greater amount up front, and the amount of spousal support decreases over time as she becomes more self-sufficient.

## Reservation of Spousal Support

A reservation of right means that spousal support isn't awarded at the time of the separation agreement or the divorce decree, but that the door is opened for future determination.

## "How much support will I receive, and what will my spousal support award look like?"

Unlike child support, there is no statewide formula for support awarded by final divorce decree; however, there are formulas used by various Courts for temporary support. If you are seeking support in the Juvenile Courts, then the Fairfax Guidelines are appropriate. Likewise, in circuit court, the Fairfax Guidelines as used pendente lite for parties whose monthly combined income is less than $10,000. (The Fairfax guideline *does not automatically* apply if the parties' combined monthly income is greater than $10,000, or for permanent – as in, not pendente lite – awards of spousal support. Though, let's be real – the Fairfax Guidelines are relevant, so you should know about them!)

The formula for the Fairfax guidelines is as follows:

A. Payor's Income x 26%%; 27% if no child support will be paid

B. Payee's Income x 58%; 50% if no child support will be paid

C. Line A minus Line B equals proposed Spousal Support

Generally, a look at the Fairfax Guideline is helpful in providing a client a range of spousal support she can expect.

The goals of the Court are different at a temporary support hearing early in the divorce versus the awarding of support in the final divorce decree. Early on in a pendente *lite* hearing where the Court has a very limited period of time to hear support witnesses and determine support, the Court's goal is to keep the situation relatively simple and to make an award either by formula like the Fairfax Guidelines or based on the income of the parties and their expenses.

Because *pendente lite* support has to be determined in a relatively short period of time, it is generally a function of weighing the income of the parties against the relative expenses.

## Is my spousal support award modifiable?

In a word? Probably.

Spousal support awards are typically governed by the specific language in the order or decree – if it exists. If a separation agreement is silent on modification, it is modifiable based on a material change in circumstances. In order for support to be non—modifiable, the agreement. Terms must explicitly say so. A support award resulting from a trial is always modifiable based on a material change of circumstances.

## Is my spousal support award terminable?

Yes. As we've already discussed, spousal support will terminate upon death, remarriage, or cohabitation in a relationship analogous to marriage for a period of one year or more.

## Equitable Distribution

How Virginia divides marital property (which includes al material possessions acquired by the parties during the marriage other than separate property) between spouses is determined by Section 20-107.3 of the Code of Virginia.

There are three basic types of property in Virginia: separate property, marital property and hybrid property. The definitions of these three types of property are very important, and your understanding of them is critical to your understanding of what you may or may not be entitled to in your divorce.

In your court case, it is up to the attorneys to identify all of the property of the marriage and then assist the Court with evidence to show whether the property is separate, hybrid or marital. The Court assumes that all property acquired during the marriage is marital, unless proven otherwise by one of the parties. The legal definitions of the types of property are as follows:

**Separate property:** Separate property is anything you earned, purchased, or acquired before the marriage, or after the date of separation. It also includes gifts you received from anyone other than your spouse, or anything that you inherited, regardless of whether you received it before, during, or after your marriage.

**Marital property:** This includes all property, not otherwise separate, acquired during the marriage regardless of the name on the title. This means that if your husband bought a boat in his name during the marriage, with funds earned during the marriage, the boat is a marital asset, even though it may be legally titled only in his name. Likewise, the gold bracelet that your husband gave you for Christmas as a gift is a marital asset, notwithstanding the fact that it was a gift from him to you. The courts view a marriage as an economic partnership, and all monetary and non-monetary benefits of the husband and wife should be shared by the parties equitably but not necessarily equally.

**Hybrid property:** This includes property that is part separate and part marital. An example of this might be that your grandmother left you some money prior to your getting married, and you kept in a separate account. When buying your first house, you took that money, along with money that you and your husband had saved during the marriage, and you deposited your inheritance into the joint checking account and then a week later you two went to closing and paid for the home. In Virginia, if you can trace the origin of the funds and show where they came from and how they were applied, then you can prove the residence is a hybrid property because part of the money came from separate funds and part of the money came from marital funds. There are several ways to determine what percentage of the residence is your separate property and what percentage of the residence is jointly held marital property. How the physical property is titled may not be as important as how the house was funded, unless there was a Deed of Gift from one spouse to both spouses or solely to the other spouse, in which case the Deed of Gift will probably be applied.

Once all the assets and debts of the marriage are identified and the nature of their identity is determined, then it may be necessary to value the assets for the purpose of equitable distribution. Different assets are valued in different ways. For instance, a car would be valued by its Blue Book value, whereas a home's value would normally be determined by an appraiser, or a couple may agree to use the city assessed value of the real estate. Experts may be called in to determine the value of antiques unless the parties agree on the value of the antiques. After the assets have been identified and they have been valued, then the Court will determine how those assets are to be distributed between the parties.

Perhaps the most difficult evaluation issue arises from the ownership of a family business or a sole proprietorship. Valuation experts are often required to value such assets, adding greatly to the expense of a divorce.

With real-estate assets, you are not only valuing the marital residence, but you may well have to value vacation homes, timeshares, and interests in rental homes.

## Retirements

In Virginia, there is a formula to divide retirements, 401(k) plans, 403(b), 403 plans and other retirement related accounts.

The critical dates are the date of marriage and the date of separation. The formula for retirements is as follows: the numerator (number on top) is the total number months that husband/wife was employed with the company during the marriage to the date of separation. The denominator (or bottom number) is the total number of months employed with the company. That is multiplied by 50% times benefit received (or amount in the account).

If you've been married for any period of time, it's fairly likely that you and your husband have retirement accounts to divide. For most people, that's a nerve-wracking thing, because the retirement accounts essentially represent everything you've worked for during your marriage and, usually, even beyond that.

There's a common misconception that, without exception, after divorce each spouse will walk away with 50% of the retirement accounts. The reality is just a teensy bit more complicated than that.

You should definitely know, ahead of time, what your marital share of the retirement accounts will look like.

First, let's take a look at the formula. Here's what it looks like:

## FORMULA

$$\frac{\text{Number of years employed during the marriage to date of separation}}{\text{Total number of years husband employed by Employer*}} \times 50\% \times \text{Amount in Retirement Account Or Amount of Monthly benefit}$$

*If husband is still employed this number is unknown and we will use "Z" for "unknown"*

So, basically, your marital share is half (or 50%, whatever you want to call it), but it's only calculated based on how long you've been married while the benefits from that particular retirement asset have been accruing. You didn't earn an interest in your husband's retirement (and, likewise, he didn't earn an interest in yours) before you got married. You won't earn an interest in your husband's retirement (and, likewise, he didn't earn an interest in yours) after you divorce.

So, although it is possible to have a total overall 50% interest in the marital retirement, it is also possible (in fact, probable), that your interest will be less than 50%.

EXAMPLE A:     $100,000 in 401K
10 years of marriage to date of separation
20 years of employment

$$\frac{10}{20} \times 50\% \times \text{amount in } 401(K)$$

$\frac{1}{2} \times \frac{1}{2} \times 100,000 =$
$.25 \times 100,000 = \$25,000$

EXAMPLE B:     3,000 Pension Payment Monthly
10 years marriage to date of separation
20 years of employment

$$\frac{10}{20} \times 50\% \times \$3,000 =$$

$5/10 \times .50 \times \$3,000 =$
$\frac{1}{2} \times .50 \times \$3,000 =$
$.25 \times \$3,000 = \$750.00$ a month

Let's look at a couple of examples.

Molly married Bill in 1990. In 1995, Bill enlisted in the Navy. In 2005, Molly and Bill separated. Then, in 2015, Bill retired from the Navy after 20 years of service.

What's Molly's interest in Bill's retirement? He was in the Navy for 20 years, but not all of those 20 years overlap with his marriage. Molly and Bill were married before he joined the Navy, so she wasn't earning an interest in his military retirement then. Molly and Bill separated before he retired from the Navy, so there's 10 years after separation where Molly wasn't earning an interest in Bill's retirement.

Molly was married to Bill in 1995, when he joined the military, and stayed married to him until 2005. So, she has ten years' worth of interest in his retirement. She gets 50% of the interest in the retirement for that ten-year period—but 0% of the interest in the 5 years before he enlisted and 5 years after they divorced that he stayed in the military. Molly's interest is 25%, because she has 50% of 10 years, and her husband ultimately served 20 years before retirement—which means, overall, that she was only married for ten out of the twenty years, and that only half of her ten was marital.

Another example . . .

Marla and Tony were married in 1990, too. Tony enlisted in the Navy in 1991. He served a full twenty years in the Navy, before he retired in 2011. Marla and Tony divorced in 2015.

What's Marla's interest in Tony's retirement? Because Marla and Tony's marriage overlapped perfectly with his dates of service, Marla has a 50% interest in his retirement. Even though she was actually married for longer, he stopped earning retirement benefits when he retired in 2011—so, likewise, Marla stopped earning an interest in it.

Marla was married to Tony from 1991 until 2011, while Tony was earning his retirement. Because the twenty years of marriage overlapped with Tony's twenty years of military service, Marla has a 50% interest.

One more example?

Jennifer married Harley in 2000. At the time, Harley had already been working for his company for five years. In 2005, Jennifer and Harley decided to divorce. Today, in 2015, Harley still works for the same company.

What's Jennifer's interest in Harley's retirement? We don't know! Until Harley retires, it's impossible to calculate Jennifer's interest. In cases like this, where the husband hasn't retired yet, we can't calculate an exact percentage of wife's interest.

So, what do we do? Instead of putting in that Jennifer has a 25% interest or a 50% interest in Harley's retirement, we'll put the retirement formula in the separation agreement. When Harley retires, we can calculate Jennifer's percentage of interest.

Jennifer's interest in Harley's retirement is a little less with every year that Harley works. Why? Because she was only married to Harley for five years while he was earning retirement benefits and, with every extra year that Harley works, her five years accounts for less of the overall percentage of retirement earned. Five years out of ten is a 25% interest (because Jennifer has half of the interest in those five years, with ten years interest overall). Five years out of twenty years, on the other hand, is only a 12.5% interest. If he works more than twenty, the percentage will continue to decline.

So, what's the bottom line? You *do* typically get 50%, but your 50% is only 50% of the marital share—which, overall, could be 50%, or, possibly, less. It depends on the length of your marriage, the length of your husband's employment, and how much of that time overlaps.

What if it's your retirement account? It works the same way.

Your retirement can be divided, just like his retirement.

The thing about retirement is that it's not really a negotiating point. You have a marital share based on the length of your marriage, the length of your (or your husband's) employment, and how much time overlaps. It's not really negotiable. If you went to court, the judge would almost certainly award you your marital share.

Some things are bargaining points. Things like spousal support are a little more discretionary, a little more up for interpretation. There's sometimes a wide range between what one side suggests to the other side, and what a judge might award if the case were to go to court. With retirement accounts, it's not like that at all.

## My husband says I'm not entitled to any of his retirement. Is that true?

Lots of times, husbands make up stories about why their wives aren't entitled to receive a portion of their retirement.

It's just not true. Regardless of how long you've been married, if any of your marriage has overlapped with his employment, you have an interest in his retirement. If you've only overlapped for a year or two, your interest is definitely small—but it still exists.

You don't have to give it up. In fact, I cannot imagine any attorney recommending that you give it up.

## I don't want him to get a share of MY retirement!

Just like you have an interest in his retirement, he has an interest in your retirement. If your retirement accounts are equal (or close to equal), you may choose to give up your share of his retirement in exchange for his giving up an interest in yours. That happens sometimes.

If you negotiate, you have a lot more freedom than if you let your case go in front of a judge. In court, the judge is going to divide the marital retirement accounts according to each party's marital share. In negotiation, though, you can propose that he give up his share in your retirement. If he agrees, then you're fine.

Retirement is one of the more stressful but least complicated aspects of divorce. The law regarding retirement accounts is very clear cut, so it's really pretty easy to determine how much you'll receive. Even if your husband hasn't retired yet and your marital share isn't that easily and immediately discernible, we can just put the formula in and establish your share later on.

There are issues such as what date one uses to value pensions and 401Ks that require more detailed discussion with your attorney.

***Taxes.*** With very few exceptions, if you have a tax question, you will probably want to talk to a tax advisor. Tax issues are nuanced and constantly changing, and a tax advisor is the best resource for finding answers to these questions.

Still, there are a couple things about taxes that a divorce attorney can tell you, and I'll tell them to you now, before you get too far along this path. It can be helpful, at the outset, to know as much as possible.

**1.** Spousal support is not taxable to you or tax deductible to him

— this is a change from the old rules!

2. Child support is the same. It's not taxable to you, if you're the one receiving it, and it's not tax deductible to you, if you're the one paying it.

3. Generally speaking, there are no taxes are owed on equitable distribution transfers.

If you get, for example, $50,000 from the sale of your house, you don't have to pay taxes on it. You've already paid taxes on whatever-it-was when you earned, purchased, or acquired it.

Otherwise, if you have a tax question, you should talk to a tax attorney! But that should be enough to get you started.

The next class of assets is personal property like dishes, lamps, televisions, and furniture. Personal property must be identified and valued before being distributed. Usually, parties are able to resolve the division of personal property on their own.

The value of personal property is not what you paid for it but rather, what it is worth on the market today. For most people, their personal property will have relatively little value. An example might be the large screen television you originally bought years ago for several thousand dollars, but now it may only be worth a few hundred dollars due to technological changes. With regard to personal property, it is always best for the couple to try to work out how they are going to share items rather than involving the Court or their attorneys. If the parties cannot come to an agreement there are methodologies used including alternating choices after flipping a coin to determine who goes first in selecting personal property.

Once the assets and liabilities are classified and valued, they then must be distributed. The parties can agree on the distribution of assets, or the court will do so. If the division of the assets and liabilities cannot be resolved by both parties the court will order the asset be sold, divided or that one person receive an asset and order the receiving party to pay to pay the non-receiving party a monetary award determined by the court.

## Custody and Visitation

Custody/visitation is the number one issue for most women who have children under the age of 18. The law of custody has gone from favoring mothers as caretaker of young children to being gender neutral. Either parent of a child starts with no presumption in his or her favor in a custody case. The court undertakes a custody decision by an analysis of a series of factors that, in their entirety, help the court determine the best interest of the child(ren). The factors that govern custody or visitation are outlined in Code of Va. § 20-124.3 reproduced here.

## Virginia Child Custody - Best Interest of the Child - Va. Code § 20-124.3

Section 20-124.3 of the Virginia Code lists a number of factors that the judge should consider in deciding what is in the child's best interests. They are as follows:

In determining best interests of a child for purposes of determining custody or visitation arrangements, including any pendente lite orders pursuant to § 20-103, the court shall consider the following:

1. The age and physical and mental condition of the child, giving due consideration to the child's changing developmental needs;

2. The age and physical and mental condition of each parent;

3. The relationship existing between each parent and each child, giving due consideration to the positive involvement with the child's life, the ability to accurately assess and meet the emotional, intellectual, and physical needs of the child;

4. The needs of the child, giving due consideration to other important relationships of the child, including but not limited to siblings, peers, and extended family members;

5. The role that each parent has played and will play in the future, in the upbringing and care of the child;

6. The propensity of each parent to actively support the child's contact and relationship with the other parent, including whether a parent has unreasonably denied the other parent access to or visitation with the child;

7. The relative willingness and demonstrated ability of each parent to maintain a close and continuing relationship with the child, and the ability of each parent to cooperate in and resolve disputes regarding matters affecting the child;

8. The reasonable preference of the child, if the court deems the child to be of reasonable intelligence, understanding, age, and experience to express such a preference;

9. Any history of (i) family abuse as that term is defined in

69

§ 16.1-228; (ii) sexual abuse; (iii) child abuse; or (iv) an act of violence, force, or threat as defined in § 19.2-152.7:1 that occurred no earlier than 10 years prior to the date a petition is filed. If the court finds such a history or act, the court may disregard the factors in subdivision 6; and

10. Such other factors as the court deems necessary and proper to the determination.

There are actually several Code sections that one should read discussing custody, visitation, relocation, and even access to a child's records. § 20-107.2, § 20-124.1 thru § 20-124.6.

There are basically two types of custody: Legal and Physical.

## Legal Custody

Legal custody determines who has the right to make major decisions affecting how the child is going to be raised. Normally, the courts award joint legal custody, which essentially means that both parents will jointly make major decisions regarding the child.

Ultimately, legal custody comes down to the responsibility to make joint decisions in three areas: non-emergency medical care, education, and religious upbringing.

Education issues involve where the child goes to school, how the child is doing in school, special education, IEPs, 504 Plans, etc. With matters of religion, the court is more limited due to Constitutional constraints. Normally, the child will continue the religious education and upbringing that was in place when the parents were living together. When there's conflict, it often comes down to each parent practicing his or her faith during his or her parenting time – unless there's a larger, more harmful issue that relates back to the 'best interests of the child' concerns.

The third subject of joint legal custody, medical care, really deals with decisions made regarding large medical expenditures or surgeries. Obviously, the child is going to the emergency room if an emergency arises, and will continue to have regular check-ups. Joint decisions would include decisions about medication, medical care or elective surgery. If one parent wants one outcome and the other one does not, then the courts may have to determine what care the child will receive.

## Joint Legal Custody

As we've already mentioned, in most cases legal custody is awarded jointly.

The court feels that these types of decisions are central to parenthood, and generally prefers that both parents have the right to weigh in with respect to important issues.

It does make decision making complicated, though. In cases where the parents disagree, no one parent's vote counts as more than the other. (After all, if it worked that way, what would be the point of calling it joint legal?) The only true tiebreaker would be the judge, so it's difficult (not to mention expensive) to disagree.

What it comes down to, in terms of your experience as a joint legal custodian, would be that if you can't agree on something either (1) you do it anyway, and wait for him to file a show cause on you for it, or (2) you don't do the thing anyway but you file in court for the judge to issue an opinion.

In either case, it's tricky! Obviously, it benefits you both to be able to reach an agreement where the kids are concerned, but that's not always possible.

## Sole Legal Custody

In a sole legal custody scenario, it would mean that only one parent has the decision-making ability with respect to non-emergency medical care, religious upbringing, and education.

That doesn't mean the sole legal custodian can do whatever she wants; she'd still be limited by whatever the court already ordered. For instance, if you have sole custody, and the court has awarded visitation, then the sole custodian is bound by the order of the court and cannot decide to move outside the jurisdiction of the court, or make other major decisions that would alter the court order without seeking a change to the court's order.

Don't get too excited, though.

Sole custody is not normally awarded, unless the parties agree, or if there is child abuse, drug abuse, or some major problem which adversely affects the child such as two parents who cannot work together for the sake of the child.

## Physical Custody

Physical custody is usually the more contentious of the two, because physical custody determines with whom the child resides.

The different types of physical custody really have more to do with the amount of time the child spends with each parent.

## Primary Physical Custody

Primary physical custody is a custodial arrangement where the non-custodial parent – the parent who has less parenting time – has 89 or fewer days (defined as 24-hour periods) during the course of a calendar year.

There's no "typical" custodial arrangement in Virginia. Parenting schedules can vary greatly because it depends on the circumstances of the family. A typical primary custody schedule would be every other weekend with a Wednesday night dinner and/or overnight, and two weeks in the summer. It's also possible that the non-custodial parent might have a larger chunk of time (like in the summer) instead of regular parenting time during the course of a month, especially if the parents live at some distance from each other.

## Shared Physical Custody

Shared physical custody is not necessarily 50/50 parenting time – but it could be. Technically, if the children have more than ninety overnight twenty four hour visits with each parent, then that is determined to be shared custody.

Shared physical custody can be alternating Thursday to Monday morning and half the summer or in a 2-2-3 or 2-5 pattern, alternating week on and week off, or something entirely customized to your unique situation.

One of the biggest issues we see is that child support is based on the amount of parenting time each parent has with the child. Under a primary physical custody scenario, child support is the maximum amount allowed under the law. In a shared physical custody scenario, it's based on a sliding scale – the more time the non-custodial parent has with the child, the less he pays in child support.

## Split Physical Custody

Another form of custody is split custody, where a different custodial arrangement applies to different children.

While the courts do not favor split custody, there are times when the children are deemed better off being split between parents. Parenting time can be scheduled so that the children living in different households can spend time together with a certain frequency each month – or not, depending on the specific circumstances.

## What is the "right" custodial arrangement?

The most important advice I suggest to women with regard to custody is to recognize that each family is different and there is no " right" custodial arrangement. What works for one family may not work for the next.

There are many issues involved in the custodial realm which need to be discussed in detail with an attorney. The issue of relocation is of concern to the courts because any such move interferes with the ability of the child to have a satisfactory relationship with the other parent.

When dealing with parenting issues, it is important for the parents to figure out how to communicate with one another in their rearranged family structure. Divorce need not be the destruction of a family relationship, but merely a rearrangement of how the family works.

With regard to relocation, the court requires that each parent give thirty days' advance written notice to the court and to the other parent if one intends to relocate or change his or her address. This is a very important provision.

Each parent has the right of access to the academic, medical, hospital, or other health records of that parent's minor child, unless it is otherwise ordered by the court for cause shown.

## Important – The Cardinal Rules about custody

1. "The best interest of the child" is the guiding principle in custody cases. Because the best interest of the child means something different to every participant in a custody trial, don't presume your point of view is the same as the judges.

2. Don't post on social media but if you do, do so carefully and be sure to update your privacy settings so your account in not public.

3. Monitor your child's social media page(s). You might be surprised what they are posting and it may be harmful to your case.

4. Always refer to the children as "our" children, not "my" children or "my" child.

5. Never, ever, ever, talk disparagingly about the child's father to, or in the presence of one of your children. If your child asks you a question and the honest answer requires you to address a less than flattering aspect of your spouse, it may be best to speak to a mental health professional about how to best respond.

6. The court knows that you and your husband may differ in your philosophies of how to raise the children. The court realizes that you have differences in how rules are enforced, how you punish the children, and how you treat the children. The court does not intend to impose one parenting style over the other, so try and communicate and work with your soon-to-be ex. If you cannot communicate with your husband about the children, then you may consider talking with a mental health expert about how to handle specific issues.

7. If you believe that you are going to be in a contested custody case, you need to see an attorney experienced in contested custody cases immediately, so this person can give you advice on what to do, and just as importantly, what not to do.

8. Courts look disapprovingly at restricting access to a child. Possibly the biggest reason a father would win custody is if the mother had custody and restricted the childs access to his father.

9. Introducing new boyfriends and girlfriends into the life of a child before being divorced is potentially dangerous and damaging to your child and therefore to your custody case. Short answer: Dont do it!

10. Unless the father is abusive, have a picture of her or his father in the childs room.

11. Never deny visitation because you have not received the child support check. In the eyes of the court, the two are unrelated and it is deemed unreasonable to deny visitation even to a nonpaying father.

12. Custody is about CHILDREN, not fault. Use words like *Co-Parenting, parenting time*, not *custody* or *visitation*, when speaking with your husband.

13. Don't ever, ever move out and leave without your children. This is a sure way to lose physical custody.

14. Dont move out with the children unless you have a detailed plan of action coordinated with your attorney and even then, you are at risk of losing physical custody.

15. If you are in a romantic relationship, do not have your romantic partner spend the night when the children are there, even if you think they dont know because they are asleep.

16. Even if your husbands weekends with the children are your first nights off in years, resist the urge to jump start your social

life and/or heal your broken heart by frequent late nights out. It will be used against you.

17. Do not let off steam by venting to your children's teachers, coaches, etc., about your ex. You do not want to appear the angry ex in court.

## Child Support

Virginia has adopted a child support model that is formulaic and is based on the number of children, the relative incomes of the parties, and the amount of parenting time that each parent has. The statutes governing child support are 20-108.1 and 20-108.2.

For purposes of determining child support, we have included a child support guideline worksheet and filled in an example of how it works under a primary physical custodial arrangement with the mother making $2000 per month and the father making $6,000 per month. In our example (see sample worksheet on page 102), the wife receives $520.00 spousal support, there are two children, and the monthly amount of healthcare coverage paid by father through his employer for just the children's portion is $150 per month. Childcare is after school and costs approximately $120 per month. Based on those factors, as worked out on the child support guidelines, child support is $1006.00. The court can deviate from the guidelines in special circumstances, but this is highly unusual.

# IN MARRIAGE AND DIVORCE: LOOK BEFORE YOU LEAP! 15 Questions To Consider Before Hiring Your Divorce Lawyer

The decision to hire a family law attorney – and if so, whom – is one of the biggest decisions you'll make in the entire divorce process.

We often tell people to focus on where they want to go, and to work backwards from there. Ask yourself what you hope to get out of the process, and then start by asking lawyers how they'd get you from where you are to where you want to be.

We find that a lot of people act first and then ask questions later. It's a tense time, so it's pretty understandable – but it's definitely going to be better for you if you take your time, ask your questions, and consider the consequences.

We find that, most of the time, tensions lessen over time, especially if good decisions are made up front.

Often, those good decisions can start with the attorney you hire.

**1.** Is the lawyer's practice focused exclusively on family law?

Choose a lawyer who exclusively, or at least primarily, practices in the area of matrimonial and family law. This is a constantly evolving, highly complex area of practice. You need in your corner, a knowledgeable and experienced lawyer, who is intimately familiar with the intricacies of divorce law and related matters. You cannot leave the welfare of your children and your future financial security in the hands of someone for whom family law is only one of a number of different areas of practice.

**2.** Is the lawyer attentive when you are talking?

It is crucial to have an initial consultation with any potential lawyer before signing a retainer agreement, whether in person, by phone, or video conference. An initial consultation is a golden opportunity to assess whether the attorney will treat you with compassion and dedication, or whether you will be just another number in his book and a faceless file stacked in the corner of his cluttered office. If the lawyer is checking his e-mails, typing away on his phone, or taking other calls during your meeting, you should go elsewhere.

**3.** Does the lawyer have an office policy ensuring the timely return of your phone calls?

Communication between attorney and client is key in any divorce action. A lawyer should be reachable by phone and e-mail. Unfortunately, many clients' biggest complaints against their divorce lawyers are that the lawyers fail to respond in a timely manner to their calls, e-mails, and other communications. Ask any lawyer you consider retaining whether there is an office policy regarding the prompt return of phone calls and emails. If the lawyer hesitates, there most likely is no such policy, and you will be frustrated to no end trying to get in touch with him or her.

**4.** Is the lawyer selective in accepting cases?

Does the lawyer you are considering accept every client that walks through the door, or does his or her practice consist of fewer, but select, clients? In order to provide dedicated and comprehensive service, an attorney owes it to existing clients to be highly selective in accepting new matters. Make sure the latter is the case with your attorney.

**5.** Is the lawyer's personality compatible with your personality?

In order to work effectively with your lawyer, you must be comfortable with him or her. Make sure that the lawyer you retain is someone with whom you can talk, to whom you can listen, and with whom you will be able to share the most intimate details of your life and finances without feeling threatened or uncomfortable in any way.

You'll need to feel you can be honest, even if honesty means you discuss your relationship, your sex life, and your finances – your attorney is only as good as you'll let her be, and she can't represent you fully or well without knowing the facts!

**6.** Does the lawyer treat you with compassion and empathy?

77

Make sure that the lawyer treats you as the unique individual that you are. A good lawyer will be eager to listen to your marital history and will make sure to fully understand your priorities and objectives without being in a rush to help you into categories or hurry you out the door.

**7.** Is the lawyer proactive?

You should hire a divorce lawyer who is able to provide you with a plan of action. This attorney should listen to you and then take charge.

**8.** Will the lawyer handle your case personally, or will your matter be delegated to an associate or paralegal?

Find out who will handle your case. Will it be the attorney with whom you are meeting during the initial consultation? If any portion of your case is going to be delegated to an associate or paralegal, you should insist on meeting that lawyer or paralegal as well. You must be completely satisfied that any other staff member working on your case is competent and experienced. This is essential.

**9.** Is the lawyer willing to attempt a negotiated settlement of your matter?

Only a small percentage of divorce cases actually go to trial. The majority of cases are settled, some on the courthouse steps on the very day of trial. A good attorney knows that there is no "winner" in a divorce or custody trial. If it is left unchecked, the process can be emotionally and financially devastating to both parties. Your attorney should, therefore, make every reasonable effort to negotiate a settlement on your behalf, while at the same time diligently preparing your case for the potentiality of a trial. Cases settle when the lawyers are prepared and dedicated.

**10.** Is the lawyer willing to educate you and to answer your questions?

Your divorce lawyer must be a good communicator and be willing to answer all of your questions. Any skilled divorce lawyer knows that educated clients are better equipped to make sound and informed decisions with regard to their and their families' futures.

**11.** Is the lawyer willing to talk to you about alternatives to traditional divorce options?

Ask your attorney about different alternatives to traditional divorce – not only litigation, but negotiation, mediation, and collaboration. Can your attorney help you if you follow a non-traditional path? Will your attorney educate you about the options available to you, and help you find the right path for you? It's not the same for every client.

Is the lawyer being honest with you, or are you being promised the sun, the moon, and the stars?

Be very wary of any lawyer who guarantees a specific result in your divorce case. All litigation is inherently risky and can be influenced by present circumstances, future developments, and the decisions and attitude of the judge. Every case has strengths and weaknesses, and your lawyer should point out both. You can trust an attorney who tells it like it is—who is candid with you about your chances of obtaining a particular outcome. You cannot trust an attorney who simply tells you what you want to hear.

12. Does the lawyer underscore that your children's best interests are your highest priorities?

No parent should ever use children as pawns in a divorce action. Your children's welfare and best interests should be your paramount priority. Any good lawyer will understand and support this objective and will caution you that manipulating your children will be devastating to them personally and to your chances of being awarded custody.

13. Does the lawyer present himself or herself well?

If you are put off by your lawyer's personal grooming, dress, behavior, or language, chances are that the judge and opposing counsel will be too. If a lawyer's office is a mess of paper, pizza boxes, and dirty clothes, the legal documents that he or she prepares on your behalf will most likely reflect that. The work product on your case will not be thoughtful, cogent, and organized either. You want an attorney who cares enough to present himself or herself, the staff, and the office in a professional manner.

14. Is the lawyer able to utilize the latest technology?

In this day and age, your lawyer should be up to date on the latest technological developments. Your lawyer should understand how computers, the internet, social media, smartphones, etc., are changing communications, relationships, and society. He or she should be aware of the implications of this. If a lawyer has chosen to remain blindly "old school" about technology, do you think he or she cares enough to stay up to date with the latest developments in the law?

*If you need to hire a divorce lawyer, be sure to do your homework and to consider these questions before signing a retainer agreement. The last thing you need during your divorce case is to waste your precious energy on disagreements with your lawyer. So, be sure to hire the right lawyer right from the start and save yourself the agony of lost time, big bills, and endless frustration.*

# Take As Much Time To Plan Your Divorce As You Did To Plan Your Wedding

## Steps to Prepare for Divorce

1. Consult an attorney about your legal rights and attend the webinar *What Women Need to Know about Divorce*. The seminars are held on the second Saturday of every month at 8:30 a.m. to 10:00am and on the third Tuesday of every month (except December) from 6:30 p.m. to 8:00 p.m. Visit our website at hoflaw.com to learn more about our monthly divorce webinars.

2. Write a narrative for your attorney, detailing the date you began living together, the date you married, your children's birth dates, previous separations, when various assets were acquired, and the separate property either of you brought into the marriage or inherited.

3. Gather information about what you own and owe. You'll need copies of financial statements, tax returns, retirement plan documents, brokerage statements and insurance policies.

4. Obtain detailed information on each retirement plan in which you and your husband have participated.

5. Decide which assets you would like to keep if you

divorce and what you are willing to give up. Consult with your accountant about the tax consequences of various options, *especially for keeping the house.*

6. Get preliminary estimates of the value of the property you own and list the debts that you owe. Pay bills and credit cards from joint funds before separation, so you don't get stuck with them later.

7. Prepare a spending history for last year from your checkbooks so you can determine future needs and decide where to cut back if necessary.

8. Before you separate, use joint funds to repair your automobile and home, buy clothes for yourself and your children, and get needed dental work and medical checkups. If you wait until after separation, those expenses will be yours alone.

9. Set aside cash reserves to use in the first few months of separation. Transfer your share of joint funds to your separate bank account.

10. Apply for credit cards in your own name. If possible, obtain credit cards with check writing privileges.

11. After separation, close joint credit card accounts, get control of both cards issued on accounts, or notify creditors that you will no longer be responsible for your husband's charges on accounts.

12. Open a separate, secret email account that you can use before you separate and while you are in the process of divorce.

13. Begin a divorce notebook in which you list all problems with impending separation and divorce. Also list each step that you take in the divorce process, including a synopsis of all telephone calls and conferences with your attorney and accountant. Keep good notes.

14. Divorce is scary, but it will be less so if you figure out the worst that could happen and decide in advance how you will deal with it. Investigate community resources that are available to you.

15. Explore your career options. Use the crisis of divorce to catapult yourself into a more satisfying future.

16. If possible, begin negotiation discussions with your husband, as calmly as possible. Find out what his hot buttons are and where he is willing to make concessions.

17. Attend family law court proceedings and talk to family and friends who have recently been through a divorce. Get a feel for the territory you will be crossing.

18. Find a good therapist or support group to help you through the months ahead. Divorce is too traumatic to go through it alone.

19. Take your time and don't rush matters. Planning for divorce is best done deliberately and slowly. This is your chance for a new beginning.

# Financial Records Every Woman Should Be Familiar With

- Net Worth Statement
- Copies of all notes signed by yourself and your husband (Include 1st and 2nd mortgages)
- Copies of any guarantees on behalf of others signed by you or your spouse
- Tax returns for the last 3 years
- Benefit statements of your employer and spouses employer (pension plan, profit sharing, 401K, IRA, etc.)
- Life insurance policies on you, your spouse and children
- Short term disability policies on you and your spouse
- Long term disability policies on you and your spouse
- Homeowners policy
- Car insurance policies
- Health insurance policies
- Long term care insurance policies
- Other insurance policies (Mortgage payment, credit life, AAA policy, cancer policy, etc.)
- All bank account statements
- All credit card statements
- All brokerage statements
- Any military benefits
- Copy of credit history (obtain from retail merchants and any other applicable agencies)

- Inventory of personal property (written and video)
- Applicable employment contracts
- Copies of buy sell agreements
- Copies of Partnership Agreements
- Inventory of lock box
- Power of Attorney for you and your spouse
- Medical Power of Attorney for Babysitters
- Durable Medical Power of Attorney for you and your spouse
- Wills
- Living Wills
- Copies of any Wills or Trusts of which you are the beneficiary
- Trusts
- Social Security Benefits Statement
- Pre-Nuptial Agreements
- Separation Agreements
- Lease Agreements
- Real Estate Contracts
- Mutual Fund statements
- Annuity Statements

# APPENDIX

**VIRGINIA: IN THE CIRCUIT COURT OF THE CITY OF VIRGINIA BEACH\*\***

JOAN A. SMITH

Plaintiff,

v.                                          **CASE NO. CL_____**

WILLIAM R. SMITH,

Defendant.

### COMPLAINT

**COMES NOW** the Plaintiff, Joan A. Smith, by counsel, and for her complaint against the Defendant, states as follows to-wit:

1. The parties are husband and wife having been lawfully married on June 20, 1995, in Virginia Beach, VA.

2. There were two children born of the marriage, namely Rebecca I. Smith, born on October 30, 1997, and Jason W. Smith, born on April 19, 1999; there were no children born to either party and adopted by the other, nor adopted by the parties.

3. The Plaintiff is a resident and bona fide domiciliary of the Commonwealth of Virginia and has been for at least six months next preceding the filing of the suit for divorce. The Defendant is a resident and bona fide domiciliary of the Commonwealth of Virginia and has

90

been for at least six months next preceding the filing of the suit for divorce.

4. The Plaintiff resides in the City of Virginia Beach and the Defendant resides in the City of Virginia Beach.

5. The parties last resided as husband and wife at 1234 Main Street in the City of Virginia Beach.

6. The Defendant is a member of the Armed Forces of the United States.

7. Both parties are of sound mind, over the age of 18 years, sui juris and neither party is incarcerated in a mental or penal institution.

8. On January 10, 2016, without just cause or provocation, the Defendant deserted the Plaintiff and the parties have been living separate and apart, uninterrupted and without marital cohabitation since that date and there is no likelihood of reconciliation.

9. That since the separation of the parties, the Defendant has continuously bothered, molested and harassed your Plaintiff to the extent that your Plaintiff's and her children's health and well-being are being impaired.

10. That the Defendant has been guilty of cruelty toward the Plaintiff, causing reasonable apprehension of bodily harm in that the Defendant, over a period of many months physically abused, threatened, humiliated and degraded the Plaintiff and subjected her to his violent and uncontrolled fits of temper, terrorizing the household; Defendant's conduct has completely deposed the Plaintiff as a wife, rendered the marital state intolerable. Specifically on December 30, 2015, Defendant pushed Plaintiff up against a wall, causing her to fall, and on January 10, 2016, Defendant threw a set of keys at Plaintiff, which struck her in the left arm, leaving a bruise. Said conduct upon the part of the Defendant is tantamount to constructive desertion, and the parties have been separated continuously since that time without interruption and without cohabitation and there is no likelihood of reconciliation.

11. That on diverse dates and locations including, but not limited to, December 29, 2015, and January 10, 2016, in Virginia Beach, Virginia, Defendant has been guilty of adultery and/or sodomy with a person not your Plaintiff, whose name is Elaine B. Rushing, said adultery having taken place at the Notel Motel, located on Paramour Lane in Virginia Beach, Virginia. This adultery and/or

sodomy has taken place within the past five years without the knowledge, consent or connivance of your Plaintiff, and the parties have lived separate and apart since * and that there is no likelihood of reconciliation.

**WHEREFORE,** and for as much as your Plaintiff is remediless, save in a Court of Equity, your Plaintiff prays that the said Defendant be made a party to these proceedings; that all proper process may be issued; that a divorce, A MENSA ET THORO, pursuant to §20-95 of the Code of Virginia, 1950, as amended, be decreed your Plaintiff, to be later merged into a divorce A VINCULO MATRIMONII ; or, in the alternative, that a divorce A VINCULO MATRIMONII be decreed to your Plaintiff on the grounds of a one year separation pursuant to § 20-91(A)(9)(a) of the Code of Virginia, 1950, as amended; that the Plaintiff be awarded attorney fees pursuant to § 20-103 to go forward with the suit both temporary and permanent, and Court costs; that the Plaintiff be awarded custody of the children born of the marriage of the parties; that the Plaintiff be awarded money for the support, maintenance, and education of said children; that the Plaintiff be awarded temporary and permanent spousal support or a reservation of right; that the Defendant be denied spousal support; that the Defendant be required to maintain health and major medical insurance on the Plaintiff and children; the Plaintiff seeks an injunction against the Defendant from bothering and harassing and otherwise interfering with the Plaintiff; that the Defendant be restrained from contacting the Plaintiff at home or at work, and from coming onto the premises where the Plaintiff lives or works; that the Defendant be restrained from discussing the divorce around the children of the marriage, and that he have no unrelated guests of the opposite sex when the children have overnight visitation with him; that Plaintiff seeks "equitable distribution" of the "marital property," monetary award, civilian or military retainer, and any other retirement pension, if any, pursuant to § 20-107.3 of the Code of Virginia and allocation of marital debt; for an injunction against the Defendant requiring that he preserve his estate so that it will be forthcoming to meet any Decree which may be made in this suit, including an injunction enjoining and restraining him from disposing of any property, marital or otherwise, without court order; that the Plaintiff be awarded exclusive use and possession of the marital residence so that she may reside there with the children; and that the Plaintiff have such further and other relief in the premises as the nature of her cause

may require or the Court in  equity may deem meet and proper.


_____

Joan A. Smith


COMMONWEALTH OF VIRGINIA
CITY OF VIRGINIA BEACH, to-wit:

Before me, the undersigned Notary Public in and for the aforesaid City and State, personally appeared *, who, after first being placed under oath, swore that the allegations contained in the foregoing Complaint are true to the best of her knowledge this ____ day of_____, 202*.


_____

Notary Public

My commission expires:_____


_____

Sheera R. Herrell, Esquire

HOFHEIMER FAMILY LAW FIRM
1604 Hilltop West Executive Center, Suite 300
Virginia Beach, Virginia 23451
Phone 757/425-5200   Fax 757/425-6100

# Sample Income and Expense Worksheet

**Monthly Income and Expenses of** _____  Date: _____

Case No. _____

| Employed By | |
| Occupation | |
| Pay Period | |
| Salary/Wage | |

**Children in Household**

| Name | Age |
|---|---|
| | |
| | |
| | |
| | |

| | |
|---|---|
| Average Gross Pay per Month - | |
| Federal income taxes - | |
| State income taxes - | |
| FICA - | |
| Health Insurance - | |
| Life Insurance - | |
| Required Retirement - | |
| Average Monthly Net Pay - | |
| Other Income - | |
| MONTHLY NET INCOME - | |

| | Household Total | Supported Children | | Household Total | Supported Children |
|---|---|---|---|---|---|
| **Household** | | | **Clothing** | | |
| Mortgage (PITI) | | | New (not Children) | | |
| Property Taxes | | | Cleaning/Laundry | | |
| Homeowner's Insurance | | | Uniforms | | |
| Repairs/Maintenance | | | **Health Expenses** | | |
| Furniture/Furnishings | | | Doctor | | |
| **Utilities** | | | Dentist | | |
| Electricity | | | Therapist | | |
| Gas/Heating Oil | | | Eyeglasses | | |
| Water/Sewer | | | Hospital | | |
| Telephone | | | Medicines | | |
| Trash | | | Other | | |
| Cable TV & Internet | | | **Dues** | | |
| **Food** | | | Professional Assoc. | | |
| Groceries | | | Social Associations | | |
| Lunches | | | Homeowner's Assoc | | |
| **Automobile** | | | **Miscellaneous** | | |
| Payment/Depreciation | | | Gifts (Xmas,Birthday) | | |
| Gasoline | | | Church/Charity | | |
| Repair/Tags, etc. | | | Entertainment | | |
| Auto Insurance | | | Vacations | | |
| Other Transportation | | | Newspaper/Magazines | | |
| Personal Property Tax | | | Disability Insurance | | |
| **Children's Expenses** | | | Life Insurance | | |
| Child Care | | | Hobbies/Pets | | |
| School Tuition | | | Personal Grooming | | |
| Lunches | | | | | |
| School Supplies | | | **Totals Per Month** | | |
| New Clothing | | | Subtotal Expenses: | | |
| Personal Grooming | | | Subtotal Debt Payments: | | |
| | | | TOTAL EXPENSES: | | |

**Fixed Debts with Payments**  Balance  Pmt/Mo

_____

_____

_____

Total Debt Payments: [ ]

**TOTAL EXPENSES of Children** [ ]

\* - These expenses are allocated to the children whose support is to be determined on a pro-rata basis; all other expenses shown are direct expenses of the supported children.

# Sample Support Worksheet

## BASIC INFORMATION

**Style:** _____ v. _____

**Complaint No.** _____

**Date:** _____

**A. Personal Information**

1. Client name: _____

2. Wife/Mother Gross Income: $ _____ Per Month ▼ = [ Mother/Wife Income ] | **Per Month**

3. Husband/Father Gross Income: $ _____ Per Year ▼ = [ Father/Husband Income ] | **Per Month**

**Income Shares**

4. Combined monthly Gross Income: [____] [____] [____]

5. Number of children: ____ Children(s) Ages

**B. Information related to spousal support**

**Spousal Support Payor**

2. Spousal Support Payor: Husband Pays SS ▼ | **Husband**

3. If the amount of spousal support is already known for this case it is: _____

4 The Spousal Guideline to be applied in calculating Spousal Support is: J&DR P/L Statutory & Fairfax ▼

Fairfax/J&DR statutory guideline used: 30%-50% 28%-58%.

**B. Information related to Child support**

(a) The custodian (Majority Custodian) is:

Custodian is Mother ▼ | Custodian is: **Mother** | Payor of CS is: **Father**

(b) If the amount of Child Support Is already known, it is: _____

(c) Work-Related Childcare _____ → Enter Custodian's Cost - For Split Custody, enter each parent's costs directly in the Split worksheet.

(d) Children's HealthCare Premium: Father Pays: [____] Mother Pays: [____]

Support of "Other Children" - If this is not to be calculated in these worksheets.

Paid by: _____ Husband / _____ Wife

Self-Employment Tax - If self-employed, 1/2 the tax may be be subtracted from income before calculating support [For self-employment incomes over $117K/Year, see note below. **]

Annual Self Employment Tax — Monthly Income Adjustment to:

Paid by: _____ Husband [____] Husband / _____ Wife [____] Wife

**D. Counsel's Name:** _____

revised 9/4/2014